Beginning React with Hooks

Greg Lim

Table of Contents

PREFACE..5

CHAPTER 1: INTRODUCTION 7

CHAPTER 2: CREATING AND USING COMPONENTS 21

CHAPTER 3: BINDINGS, PROPS, STATE AND EVENTS.........................29

CHAPTER 4: WORKING WITH COMPONENTS 41

CHAPTER 5: CONDITIONAL RENDERING..49

CHAPTER 6: BUILDING FORMS WITH HOOKS 55

CHAPTER 7: GETTING DATA FROM RESTFUL APIS WITH HOOKS 67

CHAPTER 8: C.R.U.D. WITH HOOKS 87

CHAPTER 9: CONNECTING TO AN API TO PERSIST DATA 110

ABOUT THE AUTHOR...122

PREFACE

About this book

Developed by Facebook, React is one of the leading frameworks to build efficient web user interfaces. You use small manageable components to build large-scale, data-driven websites without page reloads.

In this book, we take you on a fun, hands-on and pragmatic journey to master React Hooks from a web development point of view. You'll start building React apps using functional components within minutes. Every section is written in a bite-sized manner and straight to the point as I don't want to waste your time (and most certainly mine) on the content you don't need. In the end, you will have what it takes to develop a real-life app.

Requirements

Basic familiarity with HTML, CSS, Javascript and object-oriented programming. No prior knowledge of React is required as we start from React basics. But if you have previous experience with React class-based components, you will progress through the material faster.

Contact and Code Examples

The source codes used in this book can be found in my GitHub repository at https://github.com/greglim81.

If you have any comments or questions concerning this book to support@i-ducate.com.

CHAPTER 1: INTRODUCTION

1.1 What is React?

React is a framework released by Facebook for creating Single Page Applications (SPA). What is a Single Page Application? Most web applications are traditionally server-side applications. The server holds the business logic, stores data, and renders the website to the client. When a client clicks on a link, it sends a request to the server, and the server will handle this request and send back a response with html code which the browser will render and be viewed by the user.

The problem here is that with this approach, the server receives a lot of requests. For example, when we go to a website and click on its *Home* page, we send a request for which the server has to respond. We click on the *About* page and it sends another request, and the server responds. We click on *Blog* and it sends another request and again the server responds. Essentially, traditional websites consist of independent HTML pages and when a user navigates these pages, the browser will request and load different HTML documents.

The many requests, response incurs a lot of time and resources spent on these tasks lead to a slow feeling of web pages, whereas the apps on your mobile phone or desktop feel very fast most of the time. React wants to bring this app like feeling to the browser where we don't always have to load new pages each time there is an action from the user.

A user still clicks on various links in a SPA. However, this time, the client handles the requests on its own and will re-render the html page through Javascript, so the server is left out here if no data from the server is needed. This is much faster as we don't have to send data over the Internet. The client doesn't have to wait for the response, and the server doesn't have to render the response.

Also, in a SPA, the browser loads one HTML document and when users navigate through the site, they stay on the same page as Javascript unloads and loads different views of the app onto the same page itself. The user gets a feel that she is navigating through pages but is actually on the same HTML page. Facebook newsfeed is a good example. Other examples are Instagram or Twitter where the content gets dynamically refreshed without requiring you to refresh or navigate to a different page.

Manipulating DOM Elements Efficiently

Loading and unloading different views of the same page involve querying and manipulating DOM elements. Such DOM operations involve adding children, removing subtrees and can be really slow. This is where React addresses this shortcoming in manipulating DOM elements efficiently. React does this by updating the browser DOM for us. With React, we do not interact with the DOM directly. We instead interact with a virtual DOM which React uses to construct the actual DOM.

The virtual DOM is made up of React elements (which we specify in JSX – more about that later) which look similar to HTML elements but are actually Javascript objects. It is much faster to work with Javascript objects than with the DOM API directly. We make changes to the Javascript object (the virtual DOM) and React renders those changes for us as efficiently as possible.

Asynchronous Operations

In times when we need to get or send data from/to the server, we send a request to the server. But these are mainly restricted to initial loading and necessary server-side operations like database operations. Besides these operations, we will not frequently need to request from the server. And if we do make server requests, we do it asynchronously, which means we still re-render the page instantly to the user and then wait for the new data to arrive and incorporate it and re-render only the required view when the data arrives; thus providing a fluid experience.

Step by Step

In this book, I will teach you about React with Hooks from scratch in step by step fashion. You will build an application where you can input search terms and receive the search results via GitHub RESTful api (fig. 1.1.1).

figure 1.1.1

In the end, you will also build a real-world application with full C.R.U.D. operations (fig. 1.1.2).

To Do	Edit	Delete
finishing writing hooks chapter	Edit	Delete
play with kids	Edit	Delete
Practise Piano	Edit	Delete

Enter To Do

Add

figure 1.1.2

These are the patterns you see on a lot of real-world applications. In this book, you will learn how to implement these patterns with React Hooks.

Although this book covers techniques for developing single-page web applications with React, web browsers are not the only place React apps can run. React Native allows us to develop iOS and Android native apps with React. And in the future, there is React VR, a framework for building interactive virtual reality apps that provides 360-degree experiences. We hope that this book will provide you with a strong base that you can build applications in React even beyond the web browser.

1.2 Thinking in Components

A React app is made up of components. For example, if we want to build a storefront module like what we see on Amazon, we can divide it into three components. The search bar component, sidebar component and products component.

A React component contains a JSX template that ultimately outputs HTML elements. It has its own data and logic to control the JSX template.

Components can also contain other components. For example, in *products* component where we display a list of products, we do so using multiple *product* components. Also, in each *product* component, we can have a *rating* component (fig. 1.2.1).

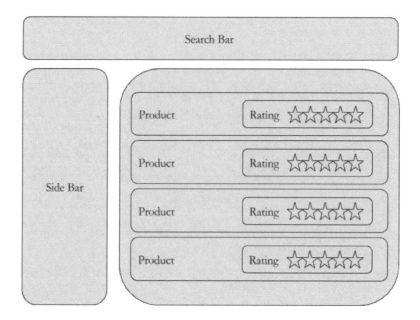

fig. 1.2.1

The benefit of such an architecture helps us to break up a large application into smaller manageable components. Plus, we can reuse components within the application or even in a different application. For example, we can re-use the rating component in a different application.

Below is an example of a component that displays a simple string 'Products'.

```
import React from 'react';

function Products() {
    return (
      <div>
        <h2>
            Products
        </h2>
      </div>
    );
}

export default Products;
```

As mentioned earlier, we define our React components using a HTML like syntax known as JSX. JSX is a syntax extension to Javascript. We use JSX to construct a virtual DOM with React elements. Facebook released JSX to provide a concise syntax for creating complex DOM trees with attributes. They hoped to make React more readable like HTML and XML.

This is the big picture of thinking in terms of components. As you progress through this book, you will see more of this in action.

1.3 Setting Up

Installing Node

First, we need to install NodeJS. NodeJS is a server-side language and we don't need it because we are not writing any server-side code. We mostly need it because of its *npm* or Node Package Manager. *npm* is very popular for managing dependencies of your applications. We will use *npm* to install other later tools that we need.

Get the latest version of NodeJS from *nodejs.org* and install it on your machine. Installing NodeJS should be pretty easy and straightforward.

To check if Node has been properly installed, type the below on your command line (Command Prompt on Windows or Terminal on Mac):

```
node -v
```

and you should see the node version displayed.

To see if npm is installed, type the below on your command line:

```
npm -v
```

and you should see the npm version displayed.

Installing Create-React-App

'*create-react-app*' is the best way to start building a new React single page application. It sets up our development environment so that we can use the latest Javascript features and optimization for our app. It is a Command Line Interface tool that makes creating a new React project, adding files and other on-going development tasks like testing, bundling and deployment easier. It uses build tools like Babel and Webpack under the hood and provides a pleasant developer experience for us that we don't have to do any manual configurations for it.

To install *'create-react-app'* from the command line, run the following:

```
npm install -g create-react-app
```

Code Editor

In this book, we will be using VScode (https://code.visualstudio.com/) which is a good, lightweight and cross-platform editor from Microsoft.

Chrome Browser

We will be using Chrome as our browser. You can use other browsers but I highly recommend you use Chrome as we will be using Chrome developer tools in this book and I want to make sure you have the same experience as we go through the coding lessons.

1.4 Creating a New Project with *create-react-app*

First, in Terminal, navigate to the folder where you want to create your React project. Next, create a new React project and skeleton application with the following command,

```
create-react-app PROJECT_NAME
```

This will create your React project folder in that directory with three dependencies: React, ReactDOM and *react-scripts*. react-scripts is created by Facebook and it installs Babel, ESLint, Webpack and more so that we don't have to configure them manually.

When the folder is created, navigate to it by typing.

```
cd PROJECT_NAME
```

Next, type

```
npm start
```

The above command launches the server, watches your files and rebuilds the app as you make changes to those files. You can also run the *npm run build* command which creates a production-ready bundle that has been transpiled and minified.

Now, navigate to http://localhost:3000/ and your app greets you with the message displayed as in fig.1.4.1.

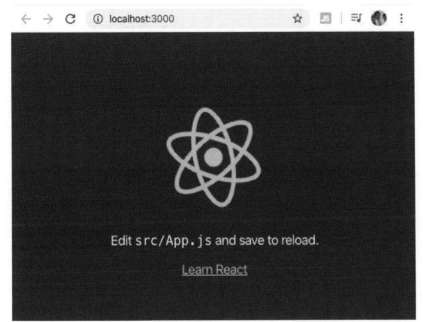

fig. 1.4.1

Alternatively

In the official documentation of *create-react-app* (https://reactjs.org/docs/create-a-new-react-app.html), it shows a different way of creating a project. I.e.:

```
npx create-react-app <project_name>
```

This is an alternate way of creating a React project without the need to run *npm install*. But do note that *npx* is a command line tool that only started to be installed in *npm* version 5.2 and higher. If you want to use *npx*, ensure that you have upgraded your node version and then run *npx*. The good thing about using *npx* is that it will automatically use the latest version of create-react-app. Other than that, there is no difference between both methods.

Project File Review

Now let's look at the project files that have been created for us. When you open the project folder in VScode editor, you will find a couple of files (fig. 1.4.2).

fig. 1.4.2

We will not go through all the files as our focus is to get started with our first React app quickly, but we will briefly go through some of the more important files and folders.

Our app lives in the *src* folder. All React components, CSS styles, images (e.g. logo.svg) and anything else our app needs goes here. Any other files outside of this folder are meant to support building your app (the app folder is where we will work 99% of the time!). In the course of this book, you will come to appreciate the uses for the rest of the library files and folders.

In the *src* folder, we have *index.js* which is the main entry point for our app. In *index.js*, we render the *App* React element into the root DOM node. Applications built with just React usually have a single root DOM node.

index.js

```
import React from 'react';
import ReactDOM from 'react-dom';
import './index.css';
import App from './App';
import * as serviceWorker from './serviceWorker';

ReactDOM.render(
  <React.StrictMode>
```

```
    <App />
  </React.StrictMode>,
  document.getElementById('root')
);


serviceWorker.unregister();
```

In *index.js*, we import both React and ReactDOM which we need to work with React in the browser. React is the library for creating views. ReactDOM is the library used to render the UI in the browser. The two libraries were split into two packages for version 0.14 and the purpose for splitting is to allow for components to be shared between the web version of React and React Native, thus supporting rendering for a variety of platforms.

index.js imports *index.css*, App component and *serviceWorker* with the following lines.

```
import './index.css';
import App from './App';
import * as serviceWorker from './serviceWorker';
```

It then renders App with:

```
ReactDOM.render(
  <React.StrictMode>
    <App />
  </React.StrictMode>,
  document.getElementById('root')
);
```

The last line `serviceWorker.unregister()` has comments:

```
// If you want your app to work offline and load faster, you can change
// unregister() to register() below. Note this comes with some pitfalls.
// Learn more about service workers: https://bit.ly/CRA-PWA
```

serviceWorker.register() is meant to create progressive web apps (PWA) catered more for mobile React Native apps to work offline. This however is out of the scope of this book and we can safely leave the code as `serviceWorker.unregister()` for now.

App.js

```
import React from 'react';
import logo from './logo.svg';
```

```
import './App.css';

function App() {
  return (
    <div className="App">
      <header className="App-header">
        <img src={logo} className="App-logo" alt="logo" />
        <p>
          Edit <code>src/App.js</code> and save to reload.
        </p>
        <a
          className="App-link"
          href="https://reactjs.org"
          target="_blank"
          rel="noopener noreferrer"
        >
          Learn React
        </a>
      </header>
    </div>
  );
}

export default App;
```

In the above, we have a function-based component called *App*. Every React application has at least one component: the root component, named *App* in *App.js*. The App component controls the view through the JSX template it returns:

```
return (
    <div className="App">
      ...
    </div>
);
```

(Note: In JSX, any element that has an HTML *class* attribute is using *className* for that property instead of *class*. Since *class* is a reserved word in Javascript, we have to use *className* to define the class attribute of an HTML element.)

A component has to return a **single** React element. In our case, *App* returns a single *<div />*. The element can be a representation of a native DOM component, such as *<div />*, or another composite component that you've defined yourself. We will dwell more on this in the next chapter.

16

The funny tag syntax returned by the component is not HTML but JSX. JSX is a syntax extension to Javascript. We use it to describe what the UI should be like. Like HTML, in JSX, an element's type is specified with a tag. The tag's attributes represent the properties. Also, the element's children can be added between the opening and closing tags.

Components can either be *function* based or *class* based. In this book, we will focus on function-based components. What we have in *App* is a function-based component as seen from its header *function App()*.

We also have the *package.json* file and *node_modules* folder:

package.json is the node package configuration which lists the third-party packages our project uses.

node_modules folder is created by Node.js and puts all third-party modules listed in *package.json* in it.

1.5 Editing our first React Component

Because our *App.js* currently has quite a bit of boilerplate code, we will delete some of the content and start with a simpler *App.js*. Open *App.js* and change it to the following:

```
import React from 'react';

function App() {
  return (
    <div>
      <h1>
        Learn React
      </h1>
    </div>
  );
}

export default App;
```

What we have above is a function-based component, as evident from the *function* declaration. The function returns a JSX template in a single React element.

With React Hooks, we can define application logic to interact with the view through state properties and adding other functions. For now, our root app component has no state properties or other functions.

When you run your app, you should see something like:

17

Learn React

Now in *App.js*, try changing "Learn React" to "Learn React Hooks". Notice that the browser reloads automatically with the revised title. Because React compiler is running in the 'watch' mode, it detects that there is a file change and re-compiles the file. In the Chrome browser, the app gets refreshed automatically so you don't have to refresh the page every time your code changes.

Function vs Class-based Components

In React, there are two primary ways of creating components, what we have shown, which is the focus of the course and which React hooks can be applied, is **function** components. The other type of component is **class** components. If you would like to learn React using class components, you can get my book at:

https://www.amazon.com/dp/B077D5212Q/

Or if you have bought this book, just drop me an email at support@i-ducate.com and I will send you a complimentary copy of my React book using class components.

For now, understand that both function and class components are still React components. That is, a component can either be implemented with a function, or with a class.

In the past, the advantages that class-based components give us include: they can access component level 'state', they provide lifecycle events e.g. *componentDidMount*, *componentDidUpdate*. These were previously very difficult or intuitive to implement with functional-based components. But with React Hooks, functional-based components can now implement all that class-components can.

And not only so, they provide other advantages like:
- Cleaner code by encapsulating logic
- Improved reusability to share logic across components
- and more.

So, it is the aim of this book that you learn to develop React apps with hooks, which would be the meaningful shift in the future for React development.

Summary

In this chapter, we have been introduced to the core building blocks of React apps which are components. We have also been introduced to the React development experience which is creating a new React project with *create-react-app*. *create-react-app* provides internal compilation which automatically generates our app for us that we can view on the browser. In the next chapter, we will begin implementing a React app.

CHAPTER 2: CREATING AND USING COMPONENTS

In the previous chapter, you learned about the core building blocks of React apps, components. In this chapter, we will implement a custom function-based component from scratch to have an idea of what it is like to build a React app.

2.1 Creating our First Component

In VScode, open the project folder that you have created in chapter 1. We first add a new file in the *src* folder and call it *Products.js* (fig. 2.1.1).

figure 2.1.1

Note the naming convention of the file; we capitalize the first letter of the component *Products* followed by *.js*.

Type out the below code into *Products.js*:

```
import React from 'react';

function Products() {
  return (
    <div>
      <h1>
        Products
```

```
      </h1>
    </div>
  );
}
```

```
export default Products;
```

Code Explanation

import React from 'react' imports the 'react' library.

In *return*, we specify the JSX that will be inserted into the DOM as HTML when the component's view is rendered. Our current html markup is:

```
<div>
  <h2>
       Products
  </h2>
</div>
```

Note that components must return a single root element. If we have:

```
return (
  <h2>
       Products
  </h2>
  <h2>
       Courses
  </h2>
)
```

The above will throw an error. So, we typically add a *<div>* to contain all internal elements like:

```
return (
  <div>
    <h2>
         Products
    </h2>
    <h2>
         Courses
    </h2>
  </div>
);
```

Lastly, *export default Products* makes this component available for other files in our application to import it.

With these simple lines of code, we have just built our first React component!

2.2 Using our Created Component

Now, go back to *App.js*. Notice that the contents of *App.js* is very similar to *Products.js*.

Remember that App component is the root of our application. It is the view component that controls our entire app or page.

Now, import and add *<Products />* to the template as shown below.

```
import React from 'react';
import Products from './Products';

function App() {
  return (
    <div>
      <h1>
        Learn React Hooks
        <Products />
      </h1>
    </div>
  );
}

export default App;
```

Code Explanation

We have just referred to another component from a component. We can also render *Products* many times:

```
    return (
      <div>
        Learn React Hooks
        <Products />
        <Products />
        <Products />
      </div>
    );
```

Now save the file and go to your browser. You should see the Products component markup displayed with the message:

Learn React Hooks

Products

Notice that we also have to first import our *Products* Component using

```
import Products from './Products';
```

For custom components that we have defined, we need to specify their path in the file system. Since App component and Products Component are in the same folder app, we use './' which means start searching from the current folder followed by the name of the component, *Products* (without *.js* extension).

<Products /> here acts as a custom tag which allows us to extend or control our virtual DOM. In this way, we can design custom components that are not part of standard JSX.

2.3 Embedding Expressions in JSX

You can embed Javascript expressions in JSX by wrapping it in curly braces. For example, we can define functions, properties and render them in the output. The below has a function *formatName* which takes in a *user* object which holds *firstName* and *lastName* properties. We then call *formatName* in *return* within the curly braces.

```
import React from 'react';

function formatName(user){
  return user.firstName + ' ' + user.lastName;
}

function App() {

  const user = {
    firstName:'Greg',
    lastName:'Lim'
  };

  return (
    <div>
      <h1>
```

```
        Hello, {formatName(user)}
      </h1>
    </div>
  );
}
```

```
export default App;
```

If the value of the property in the *user* object changes, the view will be automatically refreshed.

You can also use curly braces to embed a Javascript expression in an attribute for example:

```
function App() {

  const user = {
    firstName:'Greg',
    lastName:'Tan',
    imageUrl:'https://picsum.photos/200/300'
  };

  return (
    <div>
      <h1>
        Hello, {formatName(user)}
        <br />
        <img src={user.imageUrl}></img>
      </h1>
    </div>
  );
}
```

Displaying a List

We will illustrate using properties further by displaying a list of products in *Products*. In Products.js, add the codes shown in bold below:

```
import React from 'react';

function Products() {
    const products = ["Learning React","Pro React","Beginning React"];
    const listProducts = products.map((product) =>
        <li key={product.toString()}>{product}</li>
    );
```

```
    return (
      <div>
          <ul>{listProducts}</ul>
      </div>
    );
}

export default Products;
```

Navigate to your browser and you should see the result in fig. 2.3.1

- Learning React
- Pro React
- Beginning React

fig. 2.3.1

Code Explanation

```
    const products = ["Learning React","Pro React","Beginning React"];
```

First, in *render*, we declare an array *products* in Products Component which contain the names of the products that we are listing.

```
    const listProducts = products.map((product) =>
        <li key={product.toString()}>{product}</li>
    );
```

We next define an ES6 arrow function

```
(product) => <li key={product.toString()}>{product}</li>
```

that returns an *<li>* element for each product. We then pass in this function into *map* which loops through each element, calls the function that returns an *<li></li>* element for each product, and we are returned a new array of elements which we assign to *listProducts*.

```
    return (
      <div>
        <ul>{listProducts}</ul>
      </div>
    );
```

We include the entire *listProducts* array inside a <ul> element, and render it to the DOM:

26

Note that we have provided a *key* attribute for our list items. A "key" is a special string attribute you need to include when creating lists of elements. If you don't provide this attribute, you will still have your items listed but a warning message will be displayed. Keys help React identify which items have changed, are added, or are removed. Keys should ideally be strings that uniquely identify a list item among its siblings. Most often, you would use IDs from your data as keys. But in our case, we do not yet have an id. Thus we use the *product.toString()*. You should always use keys as much as possible because bugs creep into your code (especially when you do operations like deleting, editing individual list items – you delete/edit the wrong item!) when you do not use it.

Summary

You have learned a lot in this chapter. If you get stuck while following the code or if you would like to get the sample code we have used in this chapter, visit my GitHub repository at https://github.com/greglim81/react-hooks-chapter2 or contact me at support@i-ducate.com.

In this chapter, we created our first component. We created a Products Component that retrieves product data from an array and later renders that data on the page.

CHAPTER 3: BINDINGS, PROPS, STATE AND EVENTS

In this chapter, we will explore displaying data by binding controls in a JSX template to properties of a React component, how to apply css classes on styles dynamically, how to use the component state and how to handle events raised from DOM elements.

3.1 CSS Class Binding

In the following code, we show a button in our view using *react-bootstrap* to make our button look more professional. React-Bootstrap (https://react-bootstrap.github.io) is a library of reusable front-end components that contain JSX based templates to help build user interface components (like forms, buttons, icons) for web applications.

Installing React-Bootstrap

In the Terminal, run:

```
npm install react-bootstrap bootstrap
```

Next, in the existing project from chapter two, we need to reference *bootstrap.css*. Go to 'react-bootstrap.github.io', under 'Getting Started', 'CSS', copy the stylesheet link:

```
{/* The following line can be included in your src/index.js or App.js
file*/}

import 'bootstrap/dist/css/bootstrap.min.css';
```

and add it to *index.js* or *App.js* in your project folder to get the latest styles.

To check if we have installed react-bootstrap correctly, we add a button into our App component by adding the lines in bold:

```
import React, { Component } from 'react';
import Products from './Products';
import { Button } from 'react-bootstrap';

class App extends Component {

  render() {
```

```
    return (
      <div>
        <Products />
        <Button>Default</Button>
      </div>
    );
  }
}

export default App;
```

If you have successfully linked your react-bootstrap class, you should get your button displayed like in fig. 3.1.1.

fig. 3.1.1

There are times when we want to use different css classes on an element. For example, if we add the 'danger' button style as shown below:

```
<Button variant="danger">Default</Button>
```

we get the below button style.

And if I want to disable the button by applying the *disabled* class, I can do the following

```
<Button variant="primary" disabled>Default</Button>
```

More information of styles of *button* and other components are available at the React Bootstrap site under 'Components'.

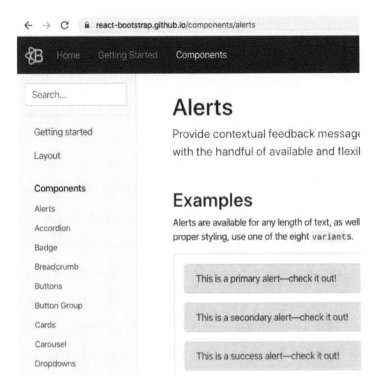

Disabling Button on Condition

Now, suppose I want to disable the button based on some condition, we can do the below:

```
function App() {
  const isValid = true;

  return (
    <div>
        <Products />
        <Button variant="danger" disabled={!isValid}>Default</Button>
    </div>
  );
}
```

That is, when *isValid = false* the *disabled* css class will be applied, making the button unclickable. If *isValid = true* the *disabled* css class will not be applied, making the button clickable.

3.2 Props

We can pass data into a component by passing in a single object called 'props'. The 'props' object contains JSX attributes. For example, suppose we want to display a list of products with its rating. We will need to assign the rating value to our rating component beforehand. We can do something like: *<Rating rating="4"/>* to display a rating of 4 stars.

'props' will contain the value of 4 assigned to the *rating* attribute. To access 'props' in our Rating component, we use *props.rating*.

For example, in *Rating.js* (our Rating component), the below code renders the rating value on the page.

```
import React from 'react';

function Rating(props) {

  return (
    <div>
        <h1>Rating: {props.rating}</h1>
    </div>
  );
}

export default Rating;
```

In *App.js*, add in the codes below into *return*:

```
function App() {
  return (
    <div>
        <Rating rating='1' />
        <Rating rating='2' />
        <Rating rating='3' />
        <Rating rating='4' />
        <Rating rating='5' />
    </div>
  );
}
```

Remember to import Rating by adding the following in App.js:

```
import Rating from './Rating';
```

If you run your app now, it should display something like:

Rating: 1

Rating: 2

Rating: 3

Rating: 4

Rating: 5

To recap, we *return* in App.js with `<Rating rating="1"/>`. React calls the Rating component with { *rating: '1'* } as the props. Our Rating component returns a `<h1>Rating: 1</h1>` element as the result and React DOM updates the DOM.

In this example, our props object contains only one attribute. But it can contain multiple and even complex objects as attribute(s). We will illustrate this later in the book.

Props are Read-Only

Note that when we access props in our components, we must never modify them. Our functions must always be 'pure' – which means that we do not attempt to change our inputs and must always return the same result for the same inputs. In other words, props are read-only. For example, the below function is impure and not allowed:

```
return (
  <div>
    <h1>Rating: {this.props.rating++}</h1>
  </div>
);
```

We can use React flexibly but it has a single strict rule: that all React components must act like pure functions concerning their props. So how do we make our application UI dynamic and change over time? Later on, we will introduce the concept of 'state', where we use it to change our output over time in response to user actions or network responses without violating this rule.

But first, we will improve the look of our rating component by showing rating stars like what we see in Amazon.com instead of showing the rating value numerically. A user can click select from a rating of one star to five stars. We will implement this as a component and reuse it in many places. For now, don't worry about calling a server or any other logic. We just want to implement the UI first.

3.3 Improving the Look

To show rating stars instead of just number values, we will use the React Icons library from https://react-icons.github.io/react-icons/ which provides popular icons in our React project. Install react icons by running:

```
npm install react-icons --save
```

We will be using the IoIosStarOutline and IoIosStar ionicons:
(https://react-icons.github.io/react-icons/icons?name=io).

IoIosStarOutline   IoIosStar

To include them in our React project, add the below codes in **bold** into Rating component:

```
import React from 'react';
import { IoIosStar, IoIosStarOutline } from 'react-icons/io'

function Rating(props) {
  return (
    <div>
        <h1>Rating: {props.rating}</h1>
        {props.rating >= 1 ? (
            <IoIosStar />
        ) : (
            <IoIosStarOutline />
        )}
        {props.rating >= 2 ? (
            <IoIosStar />
        ) : (
            <IoIosStarOutline />
        )}
        {props.rating >= 3 ? (
            <IoIosStar />
        ) : (
```

```
                    <IoIosStarOutline />
        )}
        {props.rating >= 4 ? (
            <IoIosStar />
        ) : (
            <IoIosStarOutline />
        )}
        {props.rating >= 5 ? (
            <IoIosStar />
        ) : (
            <IoIosStarOutline />
        )}
    </div>
  );
}

export default Rating;
```

Code Explanation

We first import the *IosIosStar* and *IoIosStarOutline* icons from 'react-icons/io' with

```
import { IoIosStar, IoIosStarOutline } from 'react-icons/io'
```

In the *render* method, we add the *IosIosStar* and *IoIosStarOutline* icons with:

```
        {props.rating >= 1 ? (
            <IoIosStar />
        ) : (
            <IoIosStarOutline />
        )}
```

Conditional Rendering

We conditionally render an *IosIosStar* (filled star) if *props.rating is* >= *1*. Else, render *IosIosStarOutline* (empty star). We will dwell more on the If-Else conditional code in chapter 5.

The above code is for the first star. The remaining similar repetitions are for the four remaining stars. However, note the change in value of each condition depending on which star it is. For example, the second star's condition should be

```
        {props.rating >= 2 ? (
```

```
        <IoIosStar />
    ) : (
        <IoIosStarOutline />
    ) }
```

The second star should be empty if the rating is less than two. It should be filled if the rating is more than or equal to two. The same goes for the third, fourth and fifth star.

Running your App

When we run our app, we get the icons displayed:

Rating: 1

★☆☆☆☆

Rating: 2

★★☆☆☆

Rating: 3

★★★☆☆

Rating: 4

★★★★☆

Rating: 5

★★★★★

3.4 Adding Local State to a Component

Now, suppose we want our user to be able to change the rating by clicking on the specified star. How do we make our rating component render in response to a user click? And considering that we cannot modify *props.rating*?

This is where we have to add 'state' to our Rating component. State is similar to props, but it is private and fully controlled by the component. State manages data that will change within a component. Whenever state changes, the UI is re-rendered to reflect those changes. We often refer to this as the component or local state. To add local state to our function component, we first use React Hooks' *useState* to assign an initial state:

36

```
function Rating(props) {

    const [rating, setRating] = useState(props.rating)
    ...
```

useState is a hook which we call to add some local state to a component. React preserves this state between re-renders of the component. *useState* returns an array with two values: the current state value and a function that lets you update it. In the above, we assign the current state rating value to *rating* and the function to update it to *setRating*.

(If you have experience with state in class-components, it's similar to *this.setState*, except that state in class components is a single object that contains one or more attributes. In contrast, state in function components is declared and managed per variable, i.e. *setRating*. This actually makes state related code in a function component more readable and clear about what we are updating, rather than calling *setState* in a class component. We will explore more on this later)

We initialize our initial state in `useState(props.rating)`. Our current state is a single attribute *rating* which is assigned the value from *props.rating*. You can also initialize rating in state to 0 by default with `const [rating, setRating] = useState(0)`

Next, replace *props.rating* with just *rating* in *return*:

```
    return (
        <div>
            <h1>Rating: {rating}</h1>
            {rating >= 1 ? (
                <IoIosStar />
            ) : (
                <IoIosStarOutline />
            )}
            {rating >= 2 ? (
                <IoIosStar />
            ) : (
                <IoIosStarOutline />
            )}
            {rating >= 3 ? (
                <IoIosStar />
            ) : (
                <IoIosStarOutline />
            )}
            {rating >= 4 ? (
                <IoIosStar />
            ) : (
                <IoIosStarOutline />
```

```
        ) }
        {rating >= 5 ? (
            <IoIosStar />
        ) : (
            <IoIosStarOutline />
        ) }

    </div>
    );
```

If you run your app now, it should display the Rating component just as the same as before. The purpose of why we use the local state's rating instead of *props.rating* will become more apparent in the following sections.

3.5 Handling Events with States

Next, we want to assign a rating depending on which star the user has clicked. To do so, our component needs to handle the click event. Handling events with React components is very similar to handling events on DOM elements. However, with JSX we pass a function as the event handler, rather than a string. For example, to make our rating component handle user clicks, we add the following in **bold** in the *return* method:

```
return (
    <div>
        <h1>Rating: {rating}</h1>
        {rating >= 1 ? (
            <IoIosStar onClick={() => setRating(1)}/>
        ) : (
            <IoIosStarOutline onClick={() => setRating(1)}/>
        ) }
        {rating >= 2 ? (
            <IoIosStar onClick={() => setRating(2)}/>
        ) : (
            <IoIosStarOutline onClick={() => setRating(2)}/>
        ) }
        {rating >= 3 ? (
            <IoIosStar onClick={() => setRating(3)}/>
        ) : (
            <IoIosStarOutline onClick={() => setRating(3)}/>
        ) }
        {rating >= 4 ? (
            <IoIosStar onClick={() => setRating(4)}/>
```

```
            ) : (
                <IoIosStarOutline onClick={() => setRating(4)}/>
            )}
            {rating >= 5 ? (
                <IoIosStar onClick={() => setRating(5)}/>
            ) : (
                <IoIosStarOutline onClick={() => setRating(5)}/>
            )}

        </div>
    );
```

In each star, we pass in an arrow function as the event handler with rating value to the *onClick* event. For example, we have onClick={() => setRating(1)} to assign a rating of one if a user clicks on this star. We then change the value of the argument to the arrow function depending on which star it is. The second star's *onClick* should be onClick={() => setRating(2)}. So, when a user clicks on the second star, the *setRating* method is called with property *rating* of value two. When a user clicks on the third star, the *setRating* method is called with property *rating* of value three and so on.

If you are not familiar with arrow functions, i.e. what we have in *onClick*:

```
() => setRating(5)
```

This is the same as:

```
function(){setRating(5)}
```

Many React developers declare functions in this manner thinking they result in shorter and simpler code in certain cases. In React development, we have to get used to reading and even writing our own arrow functions. In the function components we defined earlier, they can be implemented with arrow functions as well. We will cover more arrow functions in the course of this book.

Note that we CANNOT modify our state directly like *rating = 1*. Whenever we want to modify our state, we must use the state setter method we declared earlier, i.e. *setRating*

```
    const [rating, setRating] = useState(props.rating)
```

Note that whenever any setter method is called, our component automatically re-renders thus showing the updated value on to the view.

Running your App

When you run your app now, you should be able to see your ratings and also adjust their values by clicking on the specified star (figure 3.5.1).

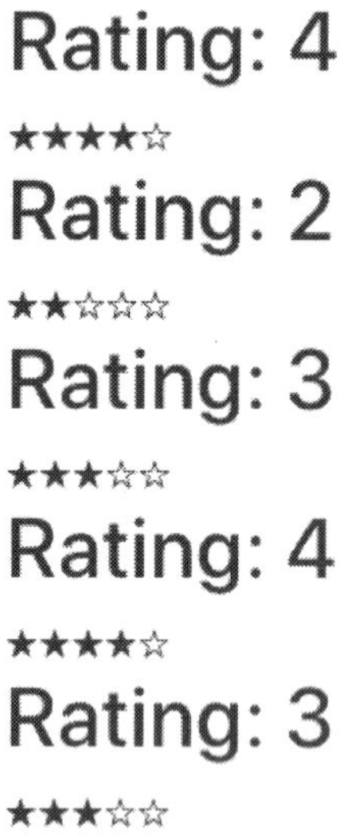

Rating: 4

★★★★☆

Rating: 2

★★☆☆☆

Rating: 3

★★★☆☆

Rating: 4

★★★★☆

Rating: 3

★★★☆☆

fig. 3.5.1

Note that we have five different rating components each having their own local state. Each updates independently. Each rating component does not affect another rating component's state.

Summary

In this chapter, we learned about CSS class binding, props, adding local state with the *useState* hook and handling events. In the next chapter, we will see how to put multiple components together in an application.

Visit my GitHub repository at https://github.com/greglim81/react-hooks-chapter3 if you have not already have the full source code for this chapter or contact me at support@i-ducate.com if you encounter any errors with your code.

CHAPTER 4: WORKING WITH COMPONENTS

In this chapter, we will learn more about using components, how to reuse them and put them together in an application. Execute the codes in the following sections in your existing project from chapter three.

4.1 Styles

On top of the components provided by React-bootstrap, we can further modify them with our own css styles required by our component. These *styles* are scoped only to your component. They won't effect to the outer DOM or other components.

To illustrate, suppose we want our filled stars to be orange, in Rating.js we add the following in **bold** after *export default Rating*.

```
...
export default Rating;

const styles={
  starStyle:{
    color: 'orange'
  }
}
```

We have created a new object under the Rating component called *styles* and in it, we provide the styling specifications. If required, you can further specify other styling properties like *height*, *backgroundColor*, *fontSize* etc.

To apply this style, add the below *style* attribute in the *<div>* containing the rating component.

```
    return (
      <div style={styles.starStyle}>
        <h1>Rating: {rating}</h1>
          ...
```

When we run our application, we will see our filled stars with the orange css applied to it (fig. 4.1.1).

★☆☆☆☆
★★☆☆☆
★★★☆☆
★★★★☆
★★★★★

figure. 4.1.1

4.2 Example Application

We will reuse the rating component that we have made and implement a product listing like in figure 4.2.1.

Product 1
May 31, 2016
★★★★☆2
Lorem ipsum dolor sit amet, consectetur adipiscing elit. Aenean porttitor, tel enim ex faucibus nulla, id rutrum ligula purus sit amet mauris.

Product 2
October 31, 2016
★★☆☆☆12
Lorem ipsum dolor sit amet, consectetur adipiscing elit. Aenean porttitor, tel enim ex faucibus nulla, id rutrum ligula purus sit amet mauris.

Product 3
July 30, 2016
★★★★★2
Lorem ipsum dolor sit amet, consectetur adipiscing elit. Aenean porttitor, tel enim ex faucibus nulla, id rutrum ligula purus sit amet mauris.

fig. 4.2.1

This is like the list of products on Amazon. For each product, we have an image, the product name, the product release date, the rating component and the number of ratings it has.

In *src*, create a new component file *Product.js* that contains the Product Component. This component will be used to render one product. To familiarize our selves with the arrow function, let's use it to define our Product component. Fill in the file with the below code.

```
import React from 'react';

const Product = () => {
  return (
    <div>
```

```
      </div>
  );
}


export default Product;
```

This is the same as:

```
function Product(){
  return (
    <div>
    </div>
  );
}
```

Now, how do we get our template to render each product listing like in figure 4.2.1? We use the *media object* in react-bootstrap. Go to react-bootstrap.github.io, in 'Layout', click on 'Media' (fig. 4.2.2) and copy the JSX markup there into the *render* method of Product Component.

Media objects

The media object helps build complex and repetitive components (e.g. blog comments, tweets, the like and more) where some media is positioned alongside content that doesn't wrap around said media. Plus, it does this with only two required classes thanks to flexbox. Below is an example of a single media object. Only two classes are required—the wrapping `Media` and the `Media.Body` around your content. Optional padding and margin can be controlled through spacing utilities.

Media Heading

Cras sit amet nibh libero, in gravida nulla. Nulla vel metus scelerisque ante sollicitudin commodo. Cras purus odio, vestibulum in vulputate at, tempus viverra turpis. Fusce condimentum nunc ac nisi vulputate fringilla. Donec lacinia congue felis in faucibus.

fig. 4.2.2

Next in *return* of Product.js, we use *props* to assign values of our product into our JSX. Type in the below codes in bold into the template.

```
    return (
      <div>
        <Media>
            <img
```

```
          width={64}
          height={64}
          className="mr-3"
          src={props.data.imageUrl}
          alt="Image"
      />
     <Media.Body>
       <h5>{props.data.productName}</h5>
       {props.data.releasedDate }
       <Rating
            rating={props.data.rating}
            numOfReviews={props.data.numOfReviews}
       />
       <p>{props.data.description}</p>
     </Media.Body>
   </Media>
 </div>
);
```

With the above code, our product component is expecting a *props data* object with the fields: *imageUrl, productName, releasedDate* and *description*.

We have also added our rating component that expects input rating and number of reviews.

```
<Rating
     rating={props.data.rating}
     numOfReviews={props.data.numOfReviews}
/>
```

Our rating component currently only has *rating-value* as input. Add *{props.numOfReviews}* at the end of *Rating.js* to display the number of reviews beside the rating stars.

Lastly in *Product.js*, make sure that you have imported *Rating* and *Media*:

```
import Rating from './Rating';
import { Media } from 'react-bootstrap';
```

Products.js

Next in *Products.js*, add a method *getProducts* that is responsible for returning a list of products. Type in the below code (or copy it from my GitHub repository https://github.com/greglim81/react-hooks-chapter4) into *Products.js*.

```
const getProducts = () => {
  return [
```

44

```
    {
        imageUrl: "http://loremflickr.com/150/150?random=1",
        productName: "Product 1",
        releasedDate: "May 31, 2016",
        description: "Lorem ipsum dolor sit amet, consectetur adipiscing elit.
Aenean porttitor, tellus laoreet venenatis facilisis, enim ex faucibus nulla, id
rutrum ligula purus sit amet mauris. ",
        rating: 4,
        numOfReviews: 2
    },
    {
        imageUrl: "http://loremflickr.com/150/150?random=2",
        productName: "Product 2",
        releasedDate: "October 31, 2016",
        description: "Lorem ipsum dolor sit amet, consectetur adipiscing elit.
Aenean porttitor, tellus laoreet venenatis facilisis, enim ex faucibus nulla, id
rutrum ligula purus sit amet mauris. ",
        rating: 2,
        numOfReviews: 12
    },
    {
        imageUrl: "http://loremflickr.com/150/150?random=3",
        productName: "Product 3",
        releasedDate: "July 30, 2016",
        description: "Lorem ipsum dolor sit amet, consectetur adipiscing elit.
Aenean porttitor, tellus laoreet venenatis facilisis, enim ex faucibus nulla, id
rutrum ligula purus sit amet mauris. ",
        rating: 5,
        numOfReviews: 2
    }];
}
```

Notice that in our class, we currently hardcode an array of product objects. Later on, we will explore how to receive data from a server.

For *imageUrl*, we use http://loremflickr.com/150/150?random=1 to render a random image 150 pixels by 150 pixels. For multiple product images, we change the query string parameter *random=2, 3,4* and so on to get a different random image.

The *getProducts* method will be called in our Products component. We return the results from *getProducts* to a *products* variable. Add the codes below in **bold** into Products.js.

Products.js

```
import React, { Component } from 'react';
import Product from './Product';

function Products() {
```

```
  const getProducts = () => {
    return [...];
  }

  const products = getProducts()

  const listProducts = products.map((product) =>
      <Product key={product.productName} data={product} />
  );

  return (
    <div>
        <ul>{listProducts}</ul>
    </div>
  );
}

export default Products;
```

The code in *return()* is similar to the one in chapter three where we loop through the names in *products* array to list them. This time however, our element is not just simple strings but an object which itself contains several Product attributes.

The function we define now returns a *<Product>* component with the product *data* object as input for each product. Each *data* object input provides Product component with values from properties *imageUrl*, *productName*, *releasedDate*, *description*, *rating* and *numOfReviews*.

We pass in this function into *map* which loops through each element, calls the function that returns a *<Product />* component for each product, and we are returned a new array of *Product* components which we assign to *listProducts*.

Note that we have provided *productName* as *key* attribute for our list items. Remember that "key" is a special string attribute which help React identify which items have changed, are added, or are removed. Because *productName* might not be unique, I will leave it to you as an exercise on how you can use *Product id* which uniquely identifies a product to be the key instead.

Lastly in *App.js*, make sure you render your *Products* component:

```
import React from 'react';
import 'bootstrap/dist/css/bootstrap.min.css';
import Products from './Products';
```

```
function App() {
  return (
    <div>
        <Products />
    </div>
  );
}

export default App;
```

Save all your files and you should have your application running fine like in figure 4.2.3.

 Product 1

May 31, 2016

★★★★☆2

Lorem ipsum dolor sit amet, consectetur adipiscing elit. Aenean porttitor, tel enim ex faucibus nulla, id rutrum ligula purus sit amet mauris.

 Product 2

October 31, 2016

★★☆☆☆12

Lorem ipsum dolor sit amet, consectetur adipiscing elit. Aenean porttitor, tel enim ex faucibus nulla, id rutrum ligula purus sit amet mauris.

 Product 3

July 30, 2016

★★★★★2

Lorem ipsum dolor sit amet, consectetur adipiscing elit. Aenean porttitor, tel enim ex faucibus nulla, id rutrum ligula purus sit amet mauris.

figure 4.2.3

Summary

In this chapter, we illustrate how to modify css styles taken from *react-bootstrap* and reusing components to put them together in our example Product Listing application.

Contact me at support@i-ducate.com if you encounter any issues or visit my GitHub repository at https://github.com/greglim81/react-hooks-chapter4 for the full source code of this chapter.

CHAPTER 5: CONDITIONAL RENDERING

In this chapter, we will explore functionality to give us more control in rendering HTML via JSX.

5.1 Inline If with && Operator

Suppose you want to show or hide part of a view depending on some condition. For example, we have earlier displayed our list of products. But if there are no products to display, we want to display a message like "No products to display" on the page. To do so, in Products.js of the existing project from chapter four, add the codes in **bold**:

```
return (
  <div>
    {listProducts.length > 0 &&
      <ul>{listProducts}</ul>
    }
    {listProducts.length == 0 &&
      <ul>No Products to display</ul>
    }
  </div>
);
```

Now when we rerun our app, we should see the products displayed as same as before. But if we comment out our hard-coded data in Products.js and return an empty array instead, we should get the following message.

No Products to display

Code Explanation

```
return (

  {listProducts.length > 0 &&
    <ul>{listProducts}</ul>
  }
```

Remember that we can embed any expression in JSX by wrapping them in curly braces. Thus, we can use the Javascript logical && operator to conditionally show *listProducts* if *listProducts.length > 0*. If the condition is true, i.e. *listProducts.length > 0* is true, the element right after && which is *<ul>{listProducts}</ul>* will appear in the output. If it is false, React will ignore and skip it.

49

The following expression however evaluates to false and therefore, we don't display the message.

```
{listProducts.length == 0 &&
   <ul>No Products to display</ul>
}
```

When we return an empty array however, "*products.length > 0*" evaluates to false and we do not render the list of products. Instead we display the "No products to display message".

Inline If-Else with Conditional Operator

The above code can also be implemented with if/else by using the Javascript conditional operator *condition ? true : false*. We have actually previously used this to conditionally render either a filled star or empty one.

```
return (
  <div>
    {listProducts.length > 0 ? (
        <ul>{listProducts}</ul>
    ) : (
      <ul>No Products to display</ul>
    )}
  </div>
);
```

Code Explanation

```
{listProducts.length > 0 ? (
    <ul>{listProducts}</ul>
) : (
  <ul>No Products to display</ul>
)}
```

The above code is saying, "If *listProducts* length is > 0, then show `<ul>{listProducts}</ul>`. Otherwise (else) show what follows ':' which is `<ul>No Products to display</ul>`.

5.2 *props.children*

Sometimes, we need to insert content into our component from the outside. For example, we want to implement a component that wraps a bootstrap jumbotron. A bootstrap jumbotron (fig. 5.2.1) as defined on getbootstrap.com is "A lightweight, flexible component that can optionally extend the entire viewport to showcase key content on your site."

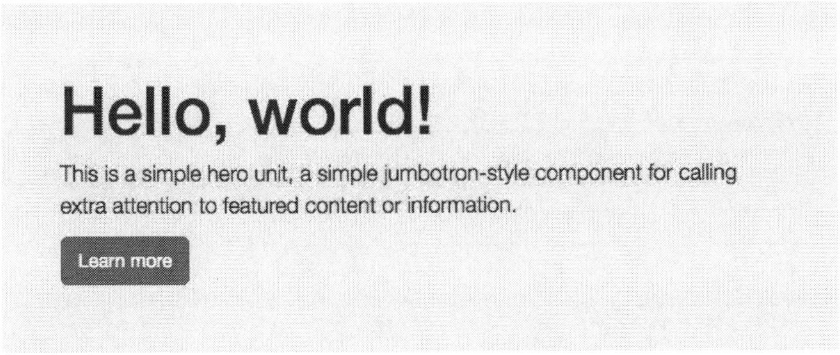

Hello, world!

This is a simple hero unit, a simple jumbotron-style component for calling extra attention to featured content or information.

Learn more

fig. 5.2.1

Here is an implementation of the bootstrap jumbotron component.

```
import React from 'react';
import { Jumbotron, Button } from 'react-bootstrap';

function JumbotronComponent() {

  return (
    <div>
        <Jumbotron>
            <h1>Hello, world!</h1>
            <p>This is a simple hero unit, a simple jumbotron-style
component for calling extra attention to featured content or
information.</p>
            <p><Button variant="primary">Learn more</Button></p>
        </Jumbotron>
    </div>
  );
}
export default JumbotronComponent;
```

The markup above can be obtained from: *https://react-bootstrap.github.io/components/jumbotron/*

The jumbotron component is called in *App.js* using,

```
import React from 'react';
import 'bootstrap/dist/css/bootstrap.min.css';

import JumbotronComponent from './JumbotronComponent';
```

```
function App() {
  return (
    <div>
        <JumbotronComponent />
    </div>
  );
}
export default App;
```

To supply content to the jumbotron component, we can use *attributes* like:

```
<JumbotronComponent body=' ...' />
```

This is not ideal however. For we probably want to write a lengthier html markup here like,

```
<JumbotronComponent>
      This is a long sentence, and I want to insert content into the
      jumbotron component from the outside.
</JumbotronComponent>
```

That is to say, we want to insert content into the jumbotron component from the outside. To do so, we use *props.children* as shown below:

```
import React from 'react';
import { Jumbotron, Button } from 'react-bootstrap';


function JumbotronComponent(props) {

  return (
    <div>
        <Jumbotron>
            <h1>Hello, world!</h1>
            <p>{props.children}</p>
            <p><Button variant="primary">Learn more</Button></p>
        </Jumbotron>
    </div>
  );
}
export default JumbotronComponent;
```

If there is a string in between an opening and closing tag, the string is passed as a special prop:

props.children. So, in the code above, *this.props.children* will be the string between *<JumboTronComponent>* and *</JumboTronComponent>* as shown in **bold** below:

```
<JumboTronComponent>
        This is a long sentence, and I want to insert content into the
        jumbotron component from the outside.
</JumboTronComponent>
```

Summary

In this chapter, we introduced the inline if '&&' operator that gives us more conditional control in rendering our JSX. We have also learned about inserting content into components from the outside using *props.children*.

Contact me at support@i-ducate.com if you encounter any issues or visit my GitHub repository at https://github.com/greglim81/react-hooks-chapter5 for the source code of *Product.js* and *JumbotronComponent.js*.

CHAPTER 6: BUILDING FORMS WITH HOOKS

In this chapter, we look at how to implement forms with validation logic in React Hooks. As an example, we will implement a login form that takes in fields *email* and *password*.

6.1 Create an Initial JSX Form Template

First, either in a new React project or in your existing project from chapter 5, create a new file *UserForm.js* and copy-paste the form template from react-bootstrap (*https://react-bootstrap.github.io/components/forms/*) into it:

```
import React from 'react';
import {Form, Button} from 'react-bootstrap'

function UserForm() {
  return (
    <div>
      <Form>
        <Form.Group controlId="formBasicEmail">
          <Form.Label>Email address</Form.Label>
          <Form.Control type="email" placeholder="Enter email" />
          <Form.Text className="text-muted">
            We'll never share your email with anyone else.
          </Form.Text>
        </Form.Group>

        <Form.Group controlId="formBasicPassword">
          <Form.Label>Password</Form.Label>
          <Form.Control type="password" placeholder="Password" />
        </Form.Group>
        <Form.Group controlId="formBasicCheckbox">
          <Form.Check type="checkbox" label="Check me out" />
        </Form.Group>
        <Button variant="primary" type="submit">
          Submit
        </Button>
      </Form>
    </div>
  );
```

```
}
export default UserForm;
```

Code Explanation

```
import {Form, Button} from 'react-bootstrap'
```

First, we import the Form and Button react-bootstrap components that will be used.

```
<Form>
  <Form.Group controlId="formBasicEmail">
    <Form.Label>Email address</Form.Label>
    <Form.Control type="email" placeholder="Enter email" />
    <Form.Text className="text-muted">
      We'll never share your email with anyone else.
    </Form.Text>
  </Form.Group>
  ...
```

Next, in *return*, under *<Form>*, we have a *<Form.Group>* component which wraps a *<Form.Label>*, *<Form.Control>* and *<Form.Text>* component. A *Form.Control* component renders an *input* (or *textarea*/*select* component if specified) with bootstrap styling. *Form.Group* provides *Form.Control* with proper spacing, along with support for a label *<Form.Label>* and help text *<Form.Text>* (fig. 6.1).

Figure 6.1

The form provides some default email validation upon submission of the form, for .e.g it has to include an '@'. We will later see how to add our own custom validation like whether it contains spaces and display alerts if the form fields have not been filled in correctly.

56

Also note that I have deleted the markup to display the form checkbox to simplify our form implementation in this chapter and focus more Hooks:

```
            <Form.Group controlId="formBasicCheckbox">
                <Form.Check type="checkbox" label="Check me out" />
            </Form.Group>
```

Handling Inputs with *useState*

In most React apps, it's convenient to have a JavaScript function that handles the submission of the form and has access to the data that the user entered into the form. And this is done by storing these user-entered data in the component state with *useState*. First, we import *useState* with:

```
import React, {useState} from 'react';
```

Next, add in the below two lines in **bold**:

```
function UserForm() {

    const [email, setEmail] = useState("")
    const [password, setPassword] = useState("")

    return (
        ...
```

That is, we declare two state variables *email* and *password* along with their state setter methods *setEmail* and *setPassword*. We set their initial value to an empty string "".

We then handle the *onChange* event that is triggered whenever a field value is changed, i.e. the user types into the form field as shown below:

```
    <Form>
        <Form.Group controlId="formBasicEmail">
        <Form.Label>Email address</Form.Label>
        <Form.Control type="email" placeholder="Enter email"
        onChange={event => setEmail(event.target.value)}/>
        <Form.Text className="text-muted">
            We'll never share your email with anyone else.
        </Form.Text>
        </Form.Group>
        ...
```

So each the user types into the form field, *onChange* of that field is called and we then call the associated handler function onChange={**event => setEmail(event.target.value)**} to set what's type into the field to *email* in state. The *event* object is provided by the browser. Through it, we can access the emitted value of the input field with *event.target.value*. Always pass functions e.g.
onChange={event => setEmail(event.target.value)}
to the handler, not the return value of the function i.e. we CAN'T do this:
onChange={setEmail(event.target.value)}

This is how we give HTML elements in JSX handler functions to respond to user interaction.

We do the same to the password field:

```
<Form.Control type="password" placeholder="Password"
onChange={event => setPassword(event.target.value)}/>
```

When we do this, we capture immediately what's entered into the form by the user. We can illustrate this by displaying the values below the form by adding:

```
    ...
    </Form>
    Email entered: {email}
    <br />
    assword entered: {password}
  </div>
...
```

When we run the app, we should see the values displayed in the bottom of the form like:

Email address

greg@greglim.com

We'll never share your email with anyone else.

Password

••••••

Submit

Email entered: greg@greglim.com
Password entered: 123456

6.5 Showing Specific Validation Errors

Currently, we have the default email validation. But we should be able to have specific validation errors depending on the input given, for example "Email is required", or "Email should be a minimum of six characters" and show corresponding validation error alerts when a user submits the form.

To show specific validation errors, we declare two more state variables to store our email and password error messages:

```
function UserForm() {

    const [email, setEmail] = useState("")
    const [password, setPassword] = useState("")
    const [emailError, setEmailError] = useState("")
    const [passwordError, setPasswordError] = useState("")

  return (
      ...
```

To handle form submission, we define a *handleSubmit* event. We then bind *handleSubmit* to the *onSubmit* event handler in the *Form* element:

```
function UserForm() {

    const [email, setEmail] = useState("")
    const [password, setPassword] = useState("")
    const [emailError, setEmailError] = useState("")
    const [passwordError, setPasswordError] = useState("")

    const handleSubmit = event => {
        event.preventDefault();
    }

    return (
        <div>
        <Form onSubmit={handleSubmit}>
      ...
```

So when the form is submitted, *handleSubmit* will be called. **event.preventDefault()** in *handleSubmit* is to ensure the page isnt' reloaded when we send the contents of the form.

In a normal app, we will want to send the form to some external API e.g. login. But before we send the network request, in *handleSubmit*, we want to perform some client-side validation. For example, if *username* length is zero, if its less then a minimum length, if there are spaces in between etc. We first illustrate this for the email field by adding the below:

```
const handleSubmit = event => {
    event.preventDefault();
    var emailValid = false;
    if(email.length == 0){
        setEmailError("Email is required");
    }
    else if(email.length < 6){
        setEmailError("Email should be minimum 6 characters");
    }
    else if(email.indexOf(' ') >= 0){
        setEmailError('Email cannot contain spaces');
    }
    else{
        setEmailError("")
        emailValid = true
    }

    if(emailValid){
        alert('Email: ' + email + '\nPassword: ' + password);
    }
}
```

That is, for each *if*-clause, we check for a specific validation, and if so, assign the specific error message to *emailError* with *setEmailError*. Only when it manages to reach the last *else* clause that we know we have no email validation errors and we set the boolean *emailValid* to true.

And if *emailValid* is true, we then show an alert with what has been entered into the form.

Running your App

Now when you run your app, fill in a valid email and password and click on submit, an alert box appears with the inputted values (fig. 6.6.1).

figure 6.6.1

In a normal app, instead of showing an alert, we will usually send the data in a request to some API. We will illustrate this in a later chapter.

Showing Validation Error Messages

Now, if we enter an invalid email address, our form doesn't submit because of the validation checks we have added in. But we should be showing validation errors to the user for her to correct her input as well. We will do that in this section.

First, import the *Alert* component from bootstrap *(https://react-bootstrap.github.io/components/alerts/)*:

```
import {Form, Button, Alert} from 'react-bootstrap'
```

Alerts provide feedback messages for user actions.

We then add the *Alert* below our input field:

```
...
    return (
        <div>
        <Form onSubmit={handleSubmit}>
            <Form.Group controlId="formBasicEmail">
            <Form.Label>Email address</Form.Label>
            <Form.Control    type="email"    placeholder="Enter    email"
onChange={event => setEmail(event.target.value)}/>
            <Form.Text className="text-muted">
                We'll never share your email with anyone else.
            </Form.Text>
```

```
</Form.Group>
{emailError.length > 0 &&
<Alert variant="danger">{emailError}</Alert>}
```
...

We wrap a condition around the *<Alert>*. We show the error message only if the error message's length is more than 0, indicating that there is an error.

Remember that the syntax '&&' is saying, if *emailError.length > 0*, then show the *Alert* component.

So if we run our app now, and submit without filling up the email field, we get:

Email address

Enter email

We'll never share your email with anyone else.

Email is required

Or if we enter an email that is less than 6 characters, we get:

Email address

g@g

We'll never share your email with anyone else.

Email should be minimum 6 characters

So you see how you can extend your application with more validation checks?

Implementing Custom Validation Exercise

In the previous example, we illustrated how to add custom validation capabilities to our application's form to fulfill our needs i.e. a valid email cannot be less than 6 characters.

As an exercise, can you try doing checking for specific validation cases for *password* and showing the custom error message on your own? If you meet with any errors, just refer to the source code at the end of the chapter.

Clearing the Fields Upon Sucessful Submit

Currently, after submitting our forms, the user-entered values in the fields remain. They should be cleared out after submission. To do so, in *handleSubmit*, after successful validation, we clear the *email* and *password* state:

```
const handleSubmit = event => {
    event.preventDefault();
  ...

    if(emailValid && passwordValid){
        alert('Email: ' + email + '\nPassword: ' + password);
        setEmail("");
        setPassword("");
    }
}
```

This still however doesn't clear our fields. We have to actually bind these state values to our fields' values:

```
        <Form.Control
        type="email"
        placeholder="Enter email"
        onChange={event => setEmail(event.target.value)}
        value={email}
    />
    ...
    <Form.Control
        type="password"
        placeholder="Password"
        onChange={event => setPassword(event.target.value)}
        value={password}
    />
```

Now, when you run your app again and submit the form, because the field values are binded to the state's, the fields will be cleared out.

Exercise

Note that we have completed our login form, try to come up with your own form and have additional inputs like text-areas, check boxes, radio buttons and more. The markup for them is available at *https://react-bootstrap.netlify.app/*. They all work similar to the input fields that we have gone through.

Complete Code

We have covered a lot about React Forms in this chapter. Below lists the complete code for *UserForm.js* which is also available in my React GitHub repository (https://github.com/greglim81/react-hooks-chapter6).

```
import React, {useState} from 'react';
import {Form, Button, Alert} from 'react-bootstrap'

function UserForm() {

    const [email, setEmail] = useState("")
    const [password, setPassword] = useState("")
    const [emailError, setEmailError] = useState("")
    const [passwordError, setPasswordError] = useState("")

    const handleSubmit = event => {
        event.preventDefault();
        var emailValid = false;
        if(email.length == 0){
            setEmailError("Email is required");
        }
        else if(email.length < 6){
            setEmailError("Email should be minimum 6 characters");
        }
        else if(email.indexOf(' ') >= 0){
            setEmailError('Email cannot contain spaces');
        }
        else{
            setEmailError("")
            emailValid = true
        }

        var passwordValid = false;
        if(password.length == 0){
            setPasswordError("Password is required");
        }
        else if(password.length < 6){
            setPasswordError("Password should be minimum 6 characters");
        }
        else if(password.indexOf(' ') >= 0){
            setPasswordError('Password cannot contain spaces');
        }
        else{
            setPasswordError("")
            passwordValid = true
        }

        if(emailValid && passwordValid){
```

```
                alert('Email: ' + email + '\nPassword: ' + password);
                setEmail("");
                setPassword("");
            }
        }

    return (
        <div>
        <Form onSubmit={handleSubmit}>
            <Form.Group controlId="formBasicEmail">
            <Form.Label>Email address</Form.Label>
            <Form.Control type="email" placeholder="Enter email" onChange={event =>
setEmail(event.target.value)} value={email}/>
            <Form.Text className="text-muted">
                We'll never share your email with anyone else.
            </Form.Text>
            </Form.Group>
            {emailError.length > 0 &&
            <Alert variant="danger">{emailError}</Alert>}

            <Form.Group controlId="formBasicPassword">
            <Form.Label>Password</Form.Label>
            <Form.Control type="password" placeholder="Password" onChange={event
=> setPassword(event.target.value)} value={password}/>
            </Form.Group>
            {passwordError.length > 0 &&
            <Alert variant="danger">{passwordError}</Alert>}
            <Button variant="primary" type="submit">
            Submit
            </Button>
        </Form>
        Email entered: {email}
        <br />
        Password entered: {password}
        </div>
    );
}
export default UserForm;
```

Summary

In this chapter, we learnt how to create a form with React Hooks. We created an initial JSX form with template from *react-bootstrap*. We then learned how to use *Form.Group*, *Form.Control* elements with *onChange* methods to handle form inputs, show form specific form field validation errors and how to validate the form upon submit.

Now after submitting a form, we need to persist the data by calling the API endpoint of the server. We will begin to explore on how to communicate with the server in the next chapter.

Visit my GitHub repository at https://github.com/greglim81/react-hooks-chapter6 if you have not already have the full source code for this chapter.

CHAPTER 7: GETTING DATA FROM RESTFUL APIS WITH HOOKS

In this chapter, we will see how to call backend services to get data through RESTful APIs with the Axios library.

7.1 GitHub RESTful API

Building RESTful APIs is beyond the scope of React because React is a client-side technology whereas building RESTful APIs require server-side technology like NodeJS, ASP.NET, Ruby on Rails and so on.

We will illustrate by connecting to the GitHub RESTful API to retrieve and manage GitHub content. You can know more about the GitHub API at

```
https://developer.github.com/v3/
```

But as a quick introduction, we can get GitHub users data with the following url,

```
https://api.github.com/search/users?q=<search term>
```

We simply specify our search term in the url to get GitHub data for user with name matching our search term. An example is shown below with search term *greg*.

```
https://api.github.com/search/users?q=greg
```

When we make a call to this url, we will get the following json objects as a result (fig. 7.1.1).

← → C ⌂ 🔒 Secure | https://**api.github.com**/search/users?q=greg

```
{
  "total_count": 14813,
  "incomplete_results": false,
  "items": [
    {
      "login": "gregkh",
      "id": 14953,
      "avatar_url": "https://avatars0.githubusercontent.com/u/14953?v=3",
      "gravatar_id": "",
      "url": "https://api.github.com/users/gregkh",
      "html_url": "https://github.com/gregkh",
      "followers_url": "https://api.github.com/users/gregkh/followers",
      "following_url": "https://api.github.com/users/gregkh/following{/other_user}",
      "gists_url": "https://api.github.com/users/gregkh/gists{/gist_id}",
      "starred_url": "https://api.github.com/users/gregkh/starred{/owner}{/repo}",
      "subscriptions_url": "https://api.github.com/users/gregkh/subscriptions",
      "organizations_url": "https://api.github.com/users/gregkh/orgs",
      "repos_url": "https://api.github.com/users/gregkh/repos",
      "events_url": "https://api.github.com/users/gregkh/events{/privacy}",
      "received_events_url": "https://api.github.com/users/gregkh/received_events",
      "type": "User",
      "site_admin": false,
      "score": 45.86066
    },
    {
      "login": "greg",
      "id": 1658846,
      "avatar_url": "https://avatars0.githubusercontent.com/u/1658846?v=3",
      "gravatar_id": "",
      "url": "https://api.github.com/users/greg",
      "html_url": "https://github.com/greg",
      "followers_url": "https://api.github.com/users/greg/followers",
      "following_url": "https://api.github.com/users/greg/following{/other_user}",
      "gists_url": "https://api.github.com/users/greg/gists{/gist_id}",
      "starred_url": "https://api.github.com/users/greg/starred{/owner}{/repo}",
      "subscriptions_url": "https://api.github.com/users/greg/subscriptions",
      "organizations_url": "https://api.github.com/users/greg/orgs",
      "repos_url": "https://api.github.com/users/greg/repos",
      "events_url": "https://api.github.com/users/greg/events{/privacy}",
      "received_events_url": "https://api.github.com/users/greg/received_events",
      "type": "User",
      "site_admin": false,
      "score": 44.028103
    },
```

fig. 7.1.1

7.2 Getting Data

To get data using a RESTful API, we are going to use the Axios library. Axios is a promise-based http client for the browser and Node.js. We use it to make ajax calls to the server.

Axios provides the *get()* method for getting a resource, *post()* for creating it, *patch()* for updating it, *delete()* for delete and *head()* for getting metadata regarding a resource. We will illustrate using Axios to get data from a RESTful API in the following code example. In chapter nine, we will illustrate using axios for post, patch and delete as well.

To begin, either create a new React project or in your existing project from chapter 6, in *src* folder, create a new file GitHub.js with the below code.

```
import React, { useEffect } from 'react';
import axios from 'axios'; // npm install axios

function GitHub() {

    useEffect(() =>{
        axios.get("https://api.github.com/search/users?q=greg")
            .then(res => {
                console.log(res.data.items);
            });
    },[])

    return (
        <div>
        </div>
    );
}
export default GitHub;
```

The code in *useEffect* will return GitHub data from our API endpoint. We will later explain what's *useEffect* and the usage of it. But we first dwell into the code inside *useEffect*.

To call our API endpoint, we need to use the *axios* library. First, install *axios* by executing the following in Terminal:

```
npm install axios
```

Then in GitHub.js, import it using

```
import axios from 'axios';
```

In *axios.get*, we call the GitHub API with argument 'greg'. *axios.get* returns a Promise which we need to subscribe to.

```
        axios.get("https://api.github.com/search/users?q=greg")
            .then(res => {
                console.log(res.data.items);
```

```
});
```

Note: If you are unfamiliar with promises, a promise allows us to make sense out of asynchronous behavior. Promises provide handlers with an asynchronous action's eventual success value. Initially, the promise is pending, and then it can either be fulfilled with a value or be rejected with an error reason. When either of these options happens, the associated handlers queued up by a promise's then method are called. This lets asynchronous methods return values like synchronous methods instead of immediately returning the final value. The asynchronous method returns a promise to supply the value at some point in the future.

In *useEffect*, we use the *get()* method of *axios* and give the url of our API endpoint. We have a search term provided by the user from an input which we will implement later. The return type of *get()* is a promise. We subscribe to this promise with *then* so that when an ajax call is completed, the response is fed to the Promise and then pushed to the component.

We then pass in our callback function *res => console.log(res.data.items)*. Note that we have to access *data.items* property to get the *items* array direct as that is the json structure of the GitHub response. So when our ajax call is completed, we print the list of items returned which is the GitHub users search results.

useEffect

Now, we come to an important question. What's *useEffect*? And why do we place our data request and retrieval code in it? As stated in reactjs.org, "If you're familiar with React class lifecycle methods, you can think of *useEffect* Hook as *componentDidMount*, *componentDidUpdate*, and *componentWillUnmount* combined."

Or if you are not familiar with React class component lifecycle methods, *useEffect* is called after our component renders. For e.g. when our GitHub component first renders, we want to make the API data request. Thus, we place our data retrieval code in it. We will dwell more into *useEffect*, but for now, let's see the results we get when we run our app.

Running our App

Before we run our app, remember that we have to import and call our GitHub component in App.js.

```
import React from 'react';
import 'bootstrap/dist/css/bootstrap.min.css';

import GitHub from './GitHub';

function App() {
  return (
```

```
    <div>
        <GitHub />
    </div>
  );
}
export default App;
```

Now run your app in Chrome. Go to 'View', 'Developer', 'Developer Tools'. Under console, you can see the following result from the console (fig. 7.2.1).

figure 7.2.1

Our requested json object is a single object containing an items array of size 30 with each item representing the data of a GitHub user.

Each *user* object has properties *avatar_url*, *html_url*, *login*, *score*, and so on (fig. 7.2.2).

```
▼Array(30) ⊡
  ▼0:
      login: "greg"
      id: 1658846
      node_id: "MDQ6VXNlcjE2NTg4NDY="
      avatar_url: "https://avatars3.githubusercontent.com/u/1658846?v=4"
      gravatar_id: ""
      url: "https://api.github.com/users/greg"
      html_url: "https://github.com/greg"
      followers_url: "https://api.github.com/users/greg/followers"
      following_url: "https://api.github.com/users/greg/following{/other_user}"
      gists_url: "https://api.github.com/users/greg/gists{/gist_id}"
      starred_url: "https://api.github.com/users/greg/starred{/owner}{/repo}"
      subscriptions_url: "https://api.github.com/users/greg/subscriptions"
      organizations_url: "https://api.github.com/users/greg/orgs"
      repos_url: "https://api.github.com/users/greg/repos"
      events_url: "https://api.github.com/users/greg/events{/privacy}"
      received_events_url: "https://api.github.com/users/greg/received_events"
```

figure 7.2.2

71

Storing Results in State

Now that we have made a successful connection to our API, let's have a state variable to store our results instead of just logging them to the console. This will let us be able to display the results to the user. Add in the following code in **bold**:

```
import React, { useEffect, useState } from 'react';
import axios from 'axios'; // npm install axios

function GitHub() {

    const [data, setData] = useState([]);

    useEffect(() =>{
        axios.get("https://api.github.com/search/users?q=greg")
            .then(res => {
                //console.log(res.data.items);
                setData(res.data.items)
            });
    },[])

    return (
        <div>
        </div>
    );
}
export default GitHub;
```

We first import the *useState* function:
```
import React, { useEffect, useState } from 'react';
```

We then declare the state variable *data*: `const [data, setData] = useState([]);`
Here, *data* is set to an initial value of an empty array, [ ]. So you see, a variable in state can be set to any type, String, Array, Boolean, Integer, Object etc.

```
        axios.get("https://api.github.com/search/users?q=greg")
            .then(res => {
                //console.log(res.data.items);
                setData(res.data.items)
            });
```

And in the callback function, instead of logging to the console, we use the state setter *setData* to assign the results to *data*.

7.3 Back to *useEffect*

What's the empty array [ ] in the 2nd argument of useEffect?

```
useEffect(() =>{
    axios.get("https://api.github.com/search/users?q=greg")
        .then(res => {
            setData(res.data.items)
        });
},[])
```

The simplest way to explain this is to remove the second argument and then re-run our app. What happens when we do so?

```
useEffect(() =>{
    axios.get("https://api.github.com/search/users?q=greg")
        .then(res => {
            setData(res.data.items)
        });
},[])
```

When *useEffect* does not have a second argument, it will be called each time *setData* is called, i.e. each time a state is changed in its body. And this results in a serious consequence because we get an infinite loop! In *useEffect*, we have *setData*, and this causes *useEffect* to be called again which calls *setData* again and this repeats in a never ending network request. So, if you try to run this in your browser, (you don't have too…), you will get something like:

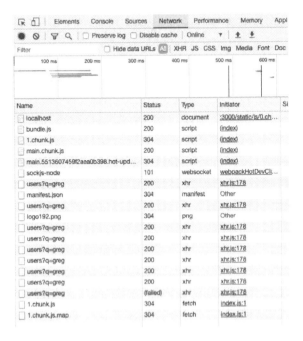

That is, multiple requests are made until GitHub itself detects a problem and blocks us! And we certainly want to avoid this situation. So, let's put back the empty array in *useEffect*.

```
useEffect(() =>{
    axios.get("https://api.github.com/search/users?q=greg")
        .then(res => {
            setData(res.data.items)
        });
}, [])
```

With the empty array in the second argument, *useEffect* is called only once when the component first renders.

In essence, without the second argument, *useEffect* is run on every render (initial render and update renders) of the component. If the 2nd argument is an empty array, *useEffect* is only called once, after the component renders for the first time.

But what if we want *useEffect* to be correctly called when the state changes? For e.g. currently out URL is hardcoded to 'greg'. What if we want *useEffect* to be called when we have a new search term?

Let's add a state property *'searchTerm'* to store a search term entered by the user. Add in the following codes in **bold**:

```
function GitHub() {
  const [data, setData] = useState([]);
  const [searchTerm, setSearchTerm] = useState("");
```

We would then append *searchTerm* to our url:

```
  useEffect(() =>{
      axios.get(`https://api.github.com/search/users?q=${searchTerm}`)
          .then(res => {
              console.log(res.data.items);
              setData(res.data.items)
          });
  },[searchTerm])
```

Note that the URL above has to be enclosed in backticks ` ` in order to append *searchTerm*.

And lastly, we specify *searchTerm* in the array of the second argument. With this, we are saying that *useEffect* should be called when the component first renders, and also each time *searchTerm* changes. In essence, if the 2nd argument contains an array of variables, if any of these variables change, *useEffect* will be called. So, in this case, the hook is not only triggered when the component is first mounted, but when one of its dependencies in the 2nd argument array is updated.

To summarize:
useEffect without a second argument, is called each time a state change occurs in its body.
useEffect with an empty array in its second argument gets called only the first time the component renders.
useEffect with a state variable in the array gets called each time the state variable changes.

We will re-visit *useEffect* again later and as we re-visit it, concepts about it using will become more apparent. For now, we will set the 2nd argument back to an empty array.

```
  useEffect(() =>{
      axios.get(`https://api.github.com/search/users?q=${searchTerm}`)
          .then(res => {
              console.log(res.data.items);
              setData(res.data.items)
          });
  },[searchTerm])
```

7.4 Showing a Loader Icon

While getting content from a server, it is often useful to show a loading icon to the user (fig. 7.4.1).

figure 7.4.1

To do so, in GitHub component, create a state variable called *isLoading* and set it to *true* like in the below code.

```
function GitHub() {

    const [data, setData] = useState([]);
    const [searchTerm, setSearchTerm] = useState("greg");
    const [isLoading, setIsLoading] = useState(true);
```

isLoading will be true when loading of results from the server is still going on. We set it to true in the beginning. We also set *searchTerm*'s initial value to 'greg'.

Next, in the *then()* method, set *isLoading* to false because at this point, we get the results from the server and loading is finished.

```
    useEffect(() =>{
        axios.get(`https://api.github.com/search/users?q=${searchTerm}`)
            .then(res => {
                setData(res.data.items)
                setIsLoading(false);
            });
    },[])
```

Lastly, in *return()*, add a *div* that shows the loading icon. We use the if && conditional to make the *div* visible only when the component is loading.

```
    return (
      <div>
        { isLoading &&
            <h4>Getting data...</h4>
        }
      </div>
    );
```

If you load your app in the browser, you should see the "Getting data" message being displayed for a short moment before data from the server is loaded.

We will now replace the "Getting data" message with the loading icon. To get the loading icon, go to *https://www.npmjs.com/package/react-loading*. *React-loading* is a library that provides many easy to use animations for React projects (fig. 7.4.2).

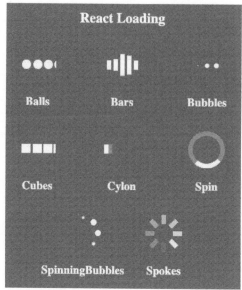

figure 7.4.2

Install the *react-loading* library in the Terminal with the code:

```
npm install react-loading
```

Back in *GitHub.js*, import *ReactLoading* with the statement:

```
import ReactLoading from 'react-loading';
```

To add the loading icon, replace the *"Getting data..."* message with the following code in bold:

```
<div>
  { isLoading &&
      <ReactLoading type="spinningBubbles" color="#444" />
  }
</div>
```

77

We use the *<ReactLoading>* tag and specify *spinningBubbles* as the type to render the spinning bubbles animation. You can try out other kinds of animations as specified in the *react-loading* documentation.

7.5 Implementing a GitHub Results Display Page

We will now implement a page which displays our GitHub user data nicely like in figure 7.5.1.

GitHub Users Results

Login: greg
Id: 1658846

Login: gregkh
Id: 14953

Login: greggman
Id: 234804

Login: gregoryyoung
Id: 381274

Login: wincent
Id: 7074

figure 7.5.1

We want to render our GitHub user data nicely. In *return()*, we use the react-bootstrap *Media Object* component from *https://react-bootstrap.github.io/layout/media/* as what we have done previously for the Product component.

We will slightly modify the markup and include it in our component as shown below:

```
function GitHub() {

    const [data, setData] = useState([]);
    const [searchTerm, setSearchTerm] = useState("");
    const [isLoading, setIsLoading] = useState(true)

    useEffect(() =>{
        axios.get("https://api.github.com/search/users?q=greg")
            .then(res => {
```

```
                setData(res.data.items)
                setIsLoading(false);
            });
    }, [])


    const listUsers = data.map((user) =>
        <Media key={user.id}>
            <a href={user.html_url}>
                <img
                    width={64}
                    height={64}
                    className="mr-3"
                    src={user.avatar_url}
                    alt="Generic placeholder"
                />
            </a>
            <Media.Body>
                <h5>Login: {user.login}</h5>
                <p>Id: { user.id }</p>
            </Media.Body>
        </Media>
    );


    return (
        <div>
            <h3>GitHub Users Results</h3>
            { isLoading &&
                <ReactLoading type="spinningBubbles" color="#444" />
            }
            {listUsers}
        </div>
    );
}
```

Lastly, import the *Media* component. Remember to install react-bootstrap if you have not done so.

```
import { Media } from 'react-bootstrap';
```

Code Explanation

```
        const listUsers = data.map((user) => <Media>...
```

We use *map* to repeat the media object for each user data we get from GitHub.

We then add Javascript JSX expressions wrapped in {} inside the template. The user's id, html_url, avatar_url and login.

```
<Media key={user.id}>
    <a href={user.html_url}>
        <img
            width={64}
            height={64}
            className="mr-3"
            src={user.avatar_url}
            alt="Generic placeholder"
        />
    </a>
    <Media.Body>
        <h5>Login: {user.login}</h5>
        <p>Id: { user.id }</p>
    </Media.Body>
</Media>
```

Finally, we display our data by including *listUsers* in our return template as shown below:

```
return (
  <div>
    <h3>GitHub Users Results</h3>
    { this.state.isLoading &&
        <ReactLoading type="spinningBubbles" color="#444" />
    }
    {listUsers}
  </div>
);
```

If you run your app now, you should get a similar page as shown below.

GitHub Users Results

Login: greg

Id: 1658846

Login: gregkh

Id: 14953

Login: greggman

Id: 234804

Login: gregoryyoung

Id: 381274

Login: wincent

Id: 7074

7.6 Adding an Input to GitHub Results Display Page

We are currently hard-coding our search term to '*greg*' in our request to GitHub. We will now make use of our *searchTerm* state so that a user can type in her search terms and retrieve the relevant search results.

Previously, we discussed about appending *searchTerm* to our url:

```
useEffect(() =>{
    axios.get(`https://api.github.com/search/users?q=${searchTerm}`)
        .then(res => {
            console.log(res.data.items);
            setData(res.data.items)
        });
},[searchTerm])
```

And specify *searchTerm* in the array of the second argument so that *useEffect* is called each time *searchTerm* changes.

Now, this however introduces another issue. Each time a user types into the keyboard and adds a character, a request is sent to the GitHub API. For e.g. if I enter 'greg', at least four requests will be sent! And if there is a typo or deletion, more requests will be sent. This floods the server with unnecessary requests, and we risk ourselves of getting blocked from the API provider. Another issue is that even before previous requests complete successfully, we send a new request, and this piles up! Get the picture?

To resolve this, two popular approaches are to use things like *debounce*, where we delay sending a request until the user has stopped typing for a pre-determined amount of time. Another approach is to have a form with an input field and submit button. In doing so, a request will only be made when the user clicks on submit. In this section, we will illustrate the form submit approach.

What we do first is to encapsulate our axios related code into a separate function which will be called both by *useEffect* and submit:

```
useEffect(() =>{
    getData();
},[])

const getData = () => {
    axios.get(`https://api.github.com/search/users?q=${searchTerm}`)
        .then(res => {
            setData(res.data.items)
            setIsLoading(false);
        });
}
```

And because no call to GitHub is made at the beginning now, we initialize *isLoading* to *false* at first as shown below:

```
const [isLoading, setIsLoading] = useState(false);
```

Once the user submits the form, we set *isLoading* to *true* just before the call to *axios.get* to show the loading icon. We thus implement *handleSubmit* as:

```
const handleSubmit = event => {
    event.preventDefault();
    setIsLoading(true);
    getData();
}
```

Once we are notified of results from the GitHub request, we set *isLoading* to *false* in *getData* to hide the loading icon.

```
const getData = () => {
    axios.get(`https://api.github.com/search/users?q=${searchTerm}`)
        .then(res => {
            setData(res.data.items)
```

```
        setIsLoading(false);
    });
}
```

Next, add the *<form>* component as shown in **bold**:

```
return (
    <div>
        <form onSubmit={handleSubmit}>
            <input
                type="text"
                onChange={event=>setSearchTerm(event.target.value)}
            />
            <button type="submit">Search</button>
        </form>
        <h3>GitHub Users Results</h3>
        { isLoading &&
            <ReactLoading type="spinningBubbles" color="#444" />
        }
        {listUsers}
    </div>
);
```

We render a simple form with a single input (fig. 7.6.1) which has an *onChange* event binded to the state's *searchTerm* property.

Running your App

greg	Search

GitHub Users Results

 Login: greg
Id: 1658846

 Login: gregkh
Id: 14953

 Login: greggman
Id: 234804

 Login: gregoryyoung
Id: 381274

 Login: wincent
Id: 7074

figure 7.6.1

When the user types in a search term and clicks 'Search', you can now see GitHub user results.

Refactoring *getData* to use *async/await*

getData is currently using a callback function. Let us refactor it to use *async/await* as shown below:

```
const getData = async() => {
    const res = await
axios.get(`https://api.github.com/search/users?q=${searchTerm}`);
    setData(res.data.items);
    setIsLoading(false);
}
```

Once we use the *await* keyword, everything reads like synchronous code. Actions after the *await* keyword are not executed until the promise resolves, meaning the code will wait.

And if we use *await*, we have to add *async* to the function declaring that it is making the request as an asynchronous function.

84

Summary

In the chapter, we learned how to implement a GitHub User Search application by connecting our React app to the GitHub RESTful API using Axios, Promises, component lifecycles and displaying a loader icon.

Visit my GitHub repository at *https://github.com/greglim81/react-hooks-chapter7* if you have not already have the full source code for this chapter.

CHAPTER 8: C.R.U.D. WITH HOOKS

Project Setup for our ToDo C.R.U.D. App

In this chapter, we will create a ToDo app using React hooks to provide functionality to create, read, update and delete todos (fig. 8.1).

To Do	Edit	Delete
Enter To Do		
Add		
finishing writing hooks chapter	Edit	Delete
play with kids	Edit	Delete
Practise Piano	Edit	Delete

Figure 8.1

In the next chapter, we will then see how to connect our app to an external API to persist our data. This app will teach you fundamentals on how to build larger and more complicated apps, in particular managing global state with React apps.

First, create a new project with:

```
npx create-react-app hooks-todos
```

Note: We can use create-react-app directly as what we have done before but using *npx* ensures that we get the latest version of *create-react-app*. Let's try it out in this project.

Next, we install the *axios* and *uuid* library with:

```
npm install axios uuid
```

We are familiar with *axios* as we have used it before. *uuid* is used to create unique id values for each of our todos.

Next, install react-bootstrap with:

```
npm install react-bootstrap bootstrap
```

Include the link to use bootstrap in *index.js*:

```
import 'bootstrap/dist/css/bootstrap.min.css';
```

Avoiding Props Drilling with React Context and the *useContext* Hook

Now, how are we going to pass values between components in our app? In React apps, we normally pass values to components through props. For example, the logged-in username in an app is often passed around since many components refer to it. Suppose we have the following *index.js*:

```
import React from 'react';
import ReactDOM from 'react-dom';
import App from './App';
import * as serviceWorker from './serviceWorker';
import 'bootstrap/dist/css/bootstrap.min.css';

const username = 'Greg'

ReactDOM.render(
  <React.StrictMode>
    <App username={username}/>
  </React.StrictMode>,
  document.getElementById('root')
);

serviceWorker.unregister();
```

From *index.js*, we pass *username* to the App component with *props*, i.e. *<App username={username}/>*

And then in *App.js*, we receive it in the *props* object:

```
function App (props){
  return <div>{props.username}</div>
}
```

We repeat the process of passing props to child components further down. For e.g.

```
function App (props){
  return (
    <Navbar username={props.username} />
  )
}
```

This process of passing data down props to the components that need them is a familiar one. It is frequently called *props drilling*. A problem results however, when the props get passed through unrelated components. For e.g. in the above example, we pass *username* from *index*, to *App*, to *Navbar*. But in *App*, it is not being used at all. Props drilling can be quite a hassle when we need to get through a number of unrelated places to their destination.

So, what's a good alternative to avoid props drilling, yet still be able to pass data around in our app?

One solution is to use React Context. React Context allows us to share values to any components in the component tree that asks for those values.

For e.g. suppose we want to share *username* around in our app. In *index.js*, we create an instance of a context and name it *UserContext*:

```
const UserContext = React.createContext(
```

Next, with *UserContext*, we set up a *provider* and put our App component between the *provider* tag:

```
...
const UserContext = React.createContext()
const username = 'Greg'

ReactDOM.render(
  <React.StrictMode>
    <UserContext.Provider value={username}>
      <App username={username}/>
    </UserContext.Provider>
  </React.StrictMode>,
  document.getElementById('root')
);
...
```

We use the *value* attribute to provide values to child components. In the above, we pass *username* into *value*.

How do we receive *username* in our App component? Now, *React.createContext()* returns an object that contains two values. The first one is *Provider* which we have just used to provide values to child components. The second one is *Consumer* which allows a child component to consume the value from Context, or in our instance, *UserContext*.

We thus first export *UserContext* in *index.js* to make it available to child components:

```
export const UserContext = React.createContext()
```

89

In *App.js*, we then import *UserContext*:

```
import { UserContext } from './index'
```

To consume *UserContext* from *App.js*, add the below code in **bold**:

```
import React from 'react';
import { UserContext } from './index';

function App (){
  return <div>
    <UserContext.Consumer>
      {value => <div>Received, {value}</div>}
    </UserContext.Consumer>
  </div>
}
export default App;
```

We consume *value* passed down from *index.js* by providing a function between the *UserContext.Consumer* tags.

If you run your app now, you should see the message rendered on your screen, 'Received, Greg'.

So, this is how we pass values down from parent components to child components without having to use *props* thus avoiding *props drilling*. Components can consume the data that's passed down through React Context's *Consumer*.

useContext Hook

However, with the introduction of React hooks, there's a new way to consume context with a hook called *useContext*.

The code to provide a context in *index.js* remains the same, However, in *App.js*, instead of using *UserContext.Consumer*, we have:

```
import React, {useContext} from 'react';
import { UserContext } from './index';

function App (){
  const value = useContext(UserContext)

  return <div>
      Received, {value}
  </div>
}
```

```
export default App;
```

When we run the above, we get the exact same result. And the code looks cleaner. We don't have to put encompassing *UserContext* elements and functions between.

That's all to using React Context with the *useContext* hook to pass data around in our app. Using *Context* instead of passing down *props*, avoid us having to navigate confusing hierarchies. We just pass the context to the *useContext* hook and get back our values from it.

Replacing Redux with the *useReducer* Hook

We have used Context to pass values around in our app. But how are we going to manage state in our app? We have shown earlier that we manage local component state using the *useState* hook. But in an app, how do we manage a global state across different components?

You might have heard of libraries like Redux to manage state across multiple components in an app. Now with the *useReducer* hook, we have available to us a lot of the functions of Redux. We can create *reducer* functions in order to manage state just like we did in Redux. Let's demonstrate with a basic counter example where we can increment, decrement or reset a count value.

First, we have to import the *useReducer* hook:

```
import React, {useReducer} from 'react';
```

We then declare our initial state:

```
const initialState = {
  count: 0
}

function App (){

...

```

We next implement a *reducer* function to implement increment, decrement and reset *count*:

```
function reducer(state, action){
  switch(action.type){
    case "increment":
      return {count : state.count + 1}
    case "decrement":
      return {count : state.count - 1}
    case "reset":
      return initialState
```

```
    default:
        return initialState
  }
}
```

reducer will take some state, and based on the action type, figure out what to do with our state. For example, if the type is 'increment', it will take the existing count in state, add one, and then return a new state with the incremented value. **We should emphasize that the existing state passed into the reducer is never modified or mutated. Rather, the reducer always returns a new state which replaces the old state.** In the following create, read, update, delete operations in our todo app, you will see that we always return a new state to replace the old state.

To use the reducer, add the following in *App.js*:

```
import { Button } from 'react-bootstrap';
...
const initialState = {
  count: 0
}

function App (){
  const [state, dispatch] = useReducer(reducer,initialState)
  return (
    <div>
      Count: {state.count}
      <br />
      <Button onClick={() => dispatch({type: 'increment'})}>
            Increment
      </Button>
      <Button variant="secondary" onClick={() => dispatch({type:
'decrement'})}>
            Decrement
      </Button>
      <Button variant="success" onClick={() => dispatch({type:
'reset'})}>
            Reset
      </Button>
    </div>
  )
}
```

Code Explanation

We first feed *reducer* and *initialState* into *useReducer*. *useReducer* then returns the current state, which we assign to *state*. It also returns *dispatch* that we use to dispatch increment, decrement and reset actions.

When we run our app, we can increment, decrement or reset our counter which will be rendered on to the view (fig. 8.2).

Figure 8.2

So all of this state management is available to us with the *useReducer* hook.

If you are lost with the code at any point, here's the counter app's full code:

App.js

```
import React, {useReducer} from 'react';
import { Button } from 'react-bootstrap';

const initialState = {
  count: 0
}

function App (){
  const [state, dispatch] = useReducer(reducer,initialState)
  return (
    <div>
      Count: {state.count}
      <br />
      <Button onClick={() => dispatch({type:
'increment'})}>Increment</Button>
      <Button variant="secondary" onClick={() => dispatch({type:
'decrement'})}>Decrement</Button>
      <Button variant="success" onClick={() => dispatch({type:
'reset'})}>Reset</Button>
    </div>
  )
}

// reducer will take some state, and based on action, it will figure out
// what to do with our state.
function reducer(state, action){
  switch(action.type){ //switch will look at our type
    case "increment":
      return {count : state.count + 1}
```

```
      case "decrement":
        return {count : state.count - 1}
      case "reset":
        return initialState
      default:
        return initialState
    }
}

export default App;
```

Combining *useContext* and *useReducer* to make Initial App State

With this understanding, we now combine *useContext* and *useReducer* to set up the initial state of our ToDo app.

In *index.js*, let's first remove the code additions we made earlier, and get back something like:

```
import React from 'react';
import ReactDOM from 'react-dom';
import App from './App';
import * as serviceWorker from './serviceWorker';
import 'bootstrap/dist/css/bootstrap.min.css';

ReactDOM.render(
  <React.StrictMode>
      <App />
  </React.StrictMode>,
  document.getElementById('root')
);

serviceWorker.unregister();
```

In *App.js*, let's also remove everything we have previously done and define our initial *todos* state:

App.js

```
import React from 'react';

const todosInitialState = {
  todos:[{ id:1, text: "finishing writing hooks chapter"},
    { id:2, text: "play with kids"},
    { id:3, text: "read bible"}
  ]
};
```

todosInitialState contains our initial state which is an array *todos*, containing three *todo* objects.

We then define our *todosReducer* function in *App.js* which currently just has a default case:

```
function todosReducer(state, action){
  switch(action.type){
    default:
      return todosInitialState
  }
}
```

And in *App.js*, we then have

```
import React, { useReducer } from 'react';
...

export const TodosContext = React.createContext()

function App (){
  const [state, dispatch] = useReducer(todosReducer,todosInitialState)

  return (
    <TodosContext.Provider value={{state,dispatch}}>
    </TodosContext.Provider>
  )
}
```

We make use of *TodosContext* to make *state* and *dispatch* available to child components.

We next create a *ToDoList* component to list out our todos. Create a new file *ToDoList.js* with the following code:

```
import React, { useContext } from 'react'
import { TodosContext } from './App'

function ToDoList(){
    // receive state and dispatch from index.js
    const {state, dispatch} = useContext(TodosContext);

    return(
        <div>
            {state.todos.map(todo =>(
                <li key={todo.id}>
                    <span>{todo.text}</span>
                </li>
```

```
        ))}
      </div>
    )
}
export default ToDoList;
```

Code Explanation

```
    const {state, dispatch} = useContext(TodosContext);
```

Using *useContext(TodosContext)*, we receive *state* and *dispatch* from *App.js*. We then proceed to *map* and list out the todo items.

Running our App

Back in *App.js*, import *ToDoList*:

```
import ToDoList from './ToDoList'
```

And include *ToDoList* in between *TodosContext*:

```
function App (){
  const [state, dispatch] = useReducer(todosReducer,todosInitialState)

  return (
    <TodosContext.Provider value={{state,dispatch}}>
      <ToDoList />
    </TodosContext.Provider>
  )
}
```

If you run your app now, you should see an initial list of *todos* displayed.

Styling our *ToDoList*

Our list of todos looks rather plain. Let's apply some styling from React bootstrap. We will use the *Table* component (https://react-bootstrap.github.io/components/table/) to list our todos in a table.

In *ToDoList.js*, add the following:

```
import { Table } from 'react-bootstrap'
...

function ToDoList(){
```

```
    const {state, dispatch} = useContext(TodosContext);

    return(
        <div>
            <Table striped bordered hover>
            <thead>
                <tr>
                <th>To Do</th>
                <th>Edit</th>
                <th>Delete</th>
                </tr>
            </thead>
            <tbody>
                {state.todos.map(todo =>(
                    <tr key={todo.id}>
                        <td>{todo.text}</td>
                        <td>Edit</td>
                        <td>Delete</td>
                    </tr>
                ))}
            </tbody>
            </Table>
        </div>
    )
}
```

Our table has three columns, the Todo text, *Edit* and *Delete* columns.

And when we run our app now, our *todos* should be nicely displayed (fig. 8.3):

To Do	Edit	Delete
finishing writing hooks chapter	Edit	Delete
play with kids	Edit	Delete
Practise Piano	Edit	Delete

Figure 8.3

Removing a Todo

Now, let's see how we remove (delete) a todo. We want to remove a todo upon clicking on 'Delete'. In the delete *td*, add the *onClick* handler:

```
<tbody>
    {state.todos.map(todo =>(
        <tr key={todo.id}>
            <td>{todo.text}</td>
            <td>Edit</td>
            <td onClick={() =>
                dispatch({type:'delete',payload:todo})}>
                Delete
            </td>
        </tr>
    ))}
</tbody>
```

The *onClick* uses *dispatch* to fire the *delete* action. We also provide a payload argument which refers to any data needed for the reducer to perform a given action (in our case, 'delete').

We next need to add to our reducer the delete case to handle the action. In *App.js*, add:

```
function todosReducer(state, action){
  switch(action.type){
    case 'delete':
      const filteredTodoState = state.todos.filter( todo => todo.id !==
action.payload.id)
      return {...state, todos: filteredTodoState}
    default:
      return todosInitialState
  }
}
```

state.todos.filter checks for each element and filters for only *todos* whose id is not equal to the todo's id in the payload (the todo to be deleted). Note that *filter* returns a whole new array for us. It does not change the existing array and then return it.

With the new filtered *todos*, we return a new state by spreading in all the current state properties with the spread operator '...' and having *todos* array now containing the new filtered *todos*. Or to put it in another manner, '…state' creates a copy of the existing state and we then assign its *todos* with *filteredTodoState*. This ensures that we return a new state, but yet having existing state properties unchanged and only *todos* changed. Remember that this is because the reducer should always return a new state to replace the old state rather than modifying the existing state.

If we run our app now, and click on 'Delete' for a todo, that todo will be removed.

Adding Todos

To let users create a todo, we will have a form on the top of our *ToDoList* component.

98

To Do	Edit	Delete
finishing writing hooks chapter	Edit	Delete
play with kids	Edit	Delete
Practise Piano	Edit	Delete

Figure 8.4

We went through forms in chapter six. So we will skip some explanations regarding implementation of a form. Add in the below codes in **bold** into *ToDoList.js*:

```
import React, { useContext, useState } from 'react'
import { TodosContext } from './App'
import { Table, Form, Button } from 'react-bootstrap'

function ToDoList(){
    const {state, dispatch} = useContext(TodosContext);
    const [todoText, setTodoText] = useState("")

    return(
        <div>
            <Form onSubmit={handleSubmit}>
                <Form.Group controlId="formBasicEmail">
                    <Form.Control
            type="text"
            placeholder="Enter To Do"
            onChange={event => setTodoText(event.target.value)}/>
                </Form.Group>
                <Button variant="primary" type="submit">
                    Submit
                </Button>
            </Form>
        <Table...>
...
```

Code Explanation

```
import { Table, Form, Button } from 'react-bootstrap'
```

We import the *Form* and *Button* component from react bootstrap to use in our form.

```
const [todoText, setTodoText] = useState("")
```

We store the user entered todo text in our component state with *useState*.

We declare a *handleSubmit* (we will add in more details later) and bind it to the Form's *onSubmit* event.

```
const handleSubmit = event => {
    event.preventDefault();
}

return(
    <div>
        <Form onSubmit={handleSubmit}>
```

In our form, we have a form input control for users to enter the todo text. In the control's *onChange*, we bind it to the function that sets the *todoText* state. These steps should be familiar to you as they are what we have gone through in chapter six.

```
<Form onSubmit={handleSubmit}>
        <Form.Group controlId="formBasicEmail">
            <Form.Control
        type="text"
        placeholder="Enter To Do"
        onChange={event => setTodoText(event.target.value)}
        value={todoText}
        />
        </Form.Group>
        <Button variant="primary" type="submit">
            Submit
        </Button>
    </Form>
```

We also bind the input control's *value* to *todoText* state so that the input control can be cleared after form submission.

Sending Dispatch in handleSubmit

Back in *handleSubmit*, we then dispatch the 'add' action with:

```
const handleSubmit = event => {
  event.preventDefault()
  dispatch({type: 'add', payload: todoText})
  setTodoText("") // to clear field after adding
```

```
}
```

Add in Reducer

Now, let's add the 'add' action type case in our *todosReducer* in *App.js*. Add in the 'add' case action as seen in the codes in **bold**:

```
import { v4 as uuidv4 } from 'uuid';
...

function todosReducer(state, action){
  switch(action.type){
    case 'add':
      const newToDo = {id: uuidv4(), text: action.payload}
      // add new todo onto array
      const addedToDos = [...state.todos,newToDo]
      // spread our state and assign todos
      return {...state,todos:addedToDos}
    case 'delete':
      const filteredTodoState = state.todos.filter( todo => todo.id !==
action.payload.id)
      return {...state, todos: filteredTodoState}
    default:
      return todosInitialState
  }
}
```

Code Explanation

```
    case 'add':
      const newToDo = {id: uuidv4(), text: action.payload}
```

We add in the 'add' case and in it, create a new todo object, *newToDo*. Using the imported *uuid* library, we assign *id* with the unique generated id. We also assign *text* with the payload from the form submit.

```
      const addedToDos = [...state.todos,newToDo]
```

We then create a new array with the existing *todos* ('...' spread operator) and adding *newToDo* to it.

```
      return {...state,todos:addedToDos}
```

We then return a new state by spreading our existing state and then assigning *addedToDos* to *todos*. By now, you should understand that we shouldn't be modifying state but instead be returning a new one. Else, the application will break.

When you run your app, you will be able to add new todos (fig. 8.5).

To Do	Edit	Delete
finishing writing hooks chapter	Edit	Delete
play with kids	Edit	Delete
read bible	Edit	Delete
Have Tea	Edit	Delete

Figure 8.5

Editing Todos

Next, we want to implement editing our todos. A user will first click on the 'Edit' of the todo she wishes to edit, and that todo text will appear in the form field for her to edit.

To do so, we add an *editMode* and *editTodo* to our *ToDoList* local component state.

```
function ToDoList(){
    const {state, dispatch} = useContext(TodosContext);
    const [todoText, setTodoText] = useState("")
    const [editMode, setEditMode] = useState(false)
    const [editTodo, setEditTodo] = useState(null)
    const buttonTitle = editMode ? "Edit" : "Add";
```

editMode will be set to true when a user clicks on a 'Edit'. *editTodo* will contain the specific todo object to be edited.

We also have a *buttonTitle* that when *editMode* is true, will be set to 'Edit', else, it will be 'Add'. This *buttonTitle* will be displayed as the button's text. So, in the Form, we render *buttonTitle* between the *Button* component.

```
<Button variant="primary" type="submit">
    {buttonTitle}
</Button>
```

Next, in 'Edit"s *onClick*, we *setTodoText* to populate the form's field with the selected todo, set *editMode* to true, and set *editTodo* in state to the selected todo.

```
<tbody>
    {state.todos.map(todo =>(
        <tr key={todo.id}>
            <td>{todo.text}</td>
            <td onClick={() => {
                setTodoText(todo.text)
                setEditMode(true)
                setEditTodo(todo)
            }}>
                Edit
            </td>
            <td onClick={() =>
                dispatch({type:'delete',payload:todo})}>
                Delete
            </td>
        </tr>
    ))}
```

```
        </tbody>
```

And then in *handleSubmit*, we make the following changes.

```
    const handleSubmit = event => {
        event.preventDefault();
        if(editMode){
            dispatch({type: 'edit', payload:{...editTodo,text:todoText}})
            setEditMode(false)
            setEditTodo(null)
        }
        else{
            dispatch({type: 'add', payload: todoText})
        }
        setTodoText("")
    }
```

We do a conditional check if *editMode* is true, we dispatch the 'edit' action with a changed todo payload *payload:{...editTodo,text:todoText}* to reflect the edited todo text. After the dispatch, we set *editMode* back to false and *editTodo* to null.

Next, we go to *App.js* and add our 'edit' action type in *todosReducer*. Add in the following code for 'edit':

```
function todosReducer(state, action){
  switch(action.type){
    case 'add':
      const newToDo = {id: uuidv4(), text: action.payload}
      const addedToDos = [...state.todos,newToDo]
      return {...state,todos:addedToDos}
    case 'delete':
      const filteredTodoState = state.todos.filter( todo => todo.id !==
action.payload.id)
      return {...state, todos: filteredTodoState}
    case 'edit':
      const updatedToDo = {...action.payload}
      const updatedToDoIndex = state.todos.findIndex(t => t.id ===
action.payload.id)
      const updatedToDos = [
        ...state.todos.slice(0,updatedToDoIndex),
        updatedToDo,
        ...state.todos.slice(updatedToDoIndex + 1)
      ];
      return {...state, todos: updatedToDos}
    default:
      return todosInitialState
  }
```

104

We first assign the payload to *updatedToDo*. Now, because there is no straightforward function to find an element and then change its content, we have to actually 'slice' up our array to get the items before and after the selected element, and in between, insert *updatedToDo*.

We first get the index of the selected element with:
const updatedToDoIndex = state.todos.findIndex(t => t.id === action.payload.id)

And to get the items before the selected element, we use *state.todos.slice(0, updatedToDoIndex)*
To get the items after the selected element, we use *state.todos.slice(updatedToDoIndex + 1)*

And to create a new array with the changed todo in between, we have:

```
const updatedToDos = [
  ...state.todos.slice(0,updatedToDoIndex),
  updatedToDo,
  ...state.todos.slice(updatedToDoIndex + 1)
];
```

When we run our app now, we can select a todo and then update its text. Congratulations if you made it thus far! In the next chapter, we will see how to persist our data by connecting to an external API.

And in case you are lost, below's the full source code. Alternatively, visit my GitHub repository at *https://github.com/greglim81/react-hooks-chapter8*.

App.js

```
import React, { useReducer} from 'react';
import ToDoList from './ToDoList'
import { v4 as uuidv4 } from 'uuid';

const todosInitialState = {
  todos:[{ id:1, text: "finishing writing hooks chapter"},
    { id:2, text: "play with kids"},
    { id:3, text: "read bible"}
  ]
};

export const TodosContext = React.createContext()

function App (){
  const [state, dispatch] = useReducer(todosReducer,todosInitialState)

  return (
    <TodosContext.Provider value={{state,dispatch}}>
      <ToDoList />
```

```
        </TodosContext.Provider>
    )
}

function todosReducer(state, action){
    switch(action.type){
        case 'add':
            const newToDo = {id: uuidv4(), text: action.payload}
            const addedToDos = [...state.todos,newToDo]
            return {...state,todos:addedToDos}
        case 'delete':
            const filteredTodoState = state.todos.filter( todo => todo.id !==
action.payload.id)
            return {...state, todos: filteredTodoState}
        case 'edit':
            const updatedToDo = {...action.payload}
            const updatedToDoIndex = state.todos.findIndex(t => t.id ===
action.payload.id)
            const updatedToDos = [
                ...state.todos.slice(0,updatedToDoIndex),
                updatedToDo,
                ...state.todos.slice(updatedToDoIndex + 1)
            ];
            return {...state, todos: updatedToDos}
        default:
            return todosInitialState
    }
}

export default App;
```

ToDoList.js

```
import React, { useContext, useState } from 'react'
import { TodosContext } from './App'
import { Table, Form, Button } from 'react-bootstrap'

function ToDoList(){
    const {state, dispatch} = useContext(TodosContext);
    const [todoText, setTodoText] = useState("")
    const [editMode, setEditMode] = useState(false)
    const [editTodo, setEditTodo] = useState(null)
    const buttonTitle = editMode ? "Edit" : "Add";

    const handleSubmit = event => {
        event.preventDefault();
        if(editMode){
```

```
            dispatch({type: 'edit', payload:
{...editTodo,text:todoText}})
            setEditMode(false)
            setEditTodo(null)
        }
        else{
            dispatch({type: 'add', payload: todoText})
        }
        setTodoText("")
    }

    return(
        <div>
            <Form onSubmit={handleSubmit}>
                <Form.Group controlId="formBasicEmail">
                    <Form.Control
                        type="text"
                        placeholder="Enter To Do"
                        onChange={event =>
setTodoText(event.target.value)}
                        value={todoText}
                    />
                </Form.Group>
                <Button variant="primary" type="submit">
                    {buttonTitle}
                </Button>
            </Form>

            <Table striped bordered hover>
            <thead>
                <tr>
                <th>To Do</th>
                <th>Edit</th>
                <th>Delete</th>
                </tr>
            </thead>
            <tbody>
                {state.todos.map(todo =>(
                    <tr key={todo.id}>
                        <td>{todo.text}</td>
                        <td onClick={() => {
                            setTodoText(todo.text)
                            setEditMode(true)
                            setEditTodo(todo)
                        }}>
                            Edit
                        </td>
```

```
                    <td onClick={() =>
dispatch({type:'delete',payload:todo})}>Delete</td>
                </tr>
            ))}
        </tbody>
        </Table>
    </div>
    )
}

export default ToDoList;
```

CHAPTER 9: CONNECTING TO AN API TO PERSIST DATA

We have made progress in our todo app. But our data is not yet persistent. That is, when we reload our application, all the changes we have done to our data is gone. In this chapter, we will connect to an API to enable persistency in create, read, update and delete todos.

The API we are connecting to can be supported by any backend, e.g. Nodejs, Firebase, ASP.Net etc. Setting up a backend is obviously beyond the scope of this book. But to quickly set up a mock API, we will use *json-server* (*https://github.com/typicode/json-server*) which makes it easy for us to set up JSON APIs for use in demos and proof of concepts.

In your Terminal, stop your React app first. Then run:

```
npm install -g json-server
```

(Note: you might need *sudo*)

Next, prepare a *todos.json* file which contains the following:

```
{
  "todos":[
      { "id":1, "text": "finishing writing hooks chapter"},
      { "id":2, "text": "play with kids"},
      { "id":3, "text": "read bible"}
  ]
}
```

These are the same *todos* we have in *App.js*:

Back in Terminal, in the folder that contains *todos.json*, run the command:

```
json-server todos.json
```

This will run a mock REST API server in your local machine and you can see the end point at:

```
http://localhost:3000/todos
```

The endpoint will return an array of *todos* just like in our initial state back in App.*js*.

Now, because *json-server* runs on port 3000 on local host, we have to change the port that our React app runs on as it currently also runs on port 3000.

In *package.json* of your react project, go to *scripts*, and add in the following in **bold**:

```
"scripts": {
    "start": "PORT=4000 react-scripts start",
    "build": "react-scripts build",
    "test": "react-scripts test",
    "eject": "react-scripts eject"
},
```

When you run *npm start* on your app, React will now run on port 4000 and won't clash with *json-server* running on port 3000.

Now that we have a mock REST API running, let's connect to it from our React app. You can imagine that the REST API is deployed on a server in a real-world scenario. Simply change the url of the endpoint to point to the server. The rest of the code remains the same.

Creating a Custom Hook to Fetch Initial App Data

Because we are retrieving our todos from the API, our initial *todos* in *App.js* will just be an empty array.

```
const todosInitialState = {
    todos:[]
};
```

We will next create a custom hook to call our API. Create a new file *useAPI.js* with the following code:

useAPI.js

```
import {useState, useEffect} from 'react'
import axios from 'axios'

const useAPI = endpoint => {
  const [data, setData] = useState([]) // initial state empty array

  //To call data when component is mounted,
  useEffect(()=> {
    getData()
  },[])

  const getData = async () => {
    const response = await axios.get(endpoint)
    setData (response.data)
```

111

```
    }

    return data;
}

export default useAPI;
```

useAPI has a state, *data* to store the data retrieved from the API. In the *getData* function, we use *axios.get* with the endpoint and then set *data* in state. Because we use *await* on *axios.get*, we need to specify *async* at the declaration of *getData*.

We apply *useEffect* with an empty array in the second argument to call *getData* when the component is mounted.

Notice that *useAPI* does not have any specific relation to *todos*. We name the results retrieved generically as *data* rather than *todos*. This is so that the custom hook can be used not just for our *todos* app, but for other API calls as well. Being in a separate file, other components can easily call *useAPI* by importing it and provide their own endpoint arguments. This illustrates how React hooks provide code reusability.

Now, in *ToDoList.js*, we will call *useAPI*. Add in the codes in **bold**:

```
import React, { useContext, useState, useEffect } from 'react'
import { TodosContext } from './App'
import { Table, Form, Button } from 'react-bootstrap'
import useAPI from './useAPI'

function ToDoList(){
    const {state, dispatch} = useContext(TodosContext);
    const [todoText, setTodoText] = useState("")
    const [editMode, setEditMode] = useState(false)
    const [editTodo, setEditTodo] = useState(null)
    const buttonTitle = editMode ? "Edit" : "Add";

    const endpoint = "http://localhost:3000/todos/"
    const savedTodos = useAPI(endpoint)

    useEffect(()=>{
        dispatch({type: "get", payload: savedTodos})
    },[savedTodos]) // dispatch whoever savedTodos changes
```

We import *useState* and *useEffect*. We also import *useAPI* and call *useAPI* with the endpoint and assign the results to *savedTodos*.

In *useEffect*, we then dispatch the *get* action with *savedTodos* as the payload:

In *App.js*, in *todosReducer*, we add the case for "get":

```
function todosReducer(state, action){
  switch(action.type){
    case 'get':
      return {...state,todos:action.payload}
    case 'add':
      const newToDo = {id: uuidv4(), text: action.payload}
      const addedToDos = [...state.todos,newToDo]
      return {...state,todos:addedToDos}
...
```

When we run our app, we retrieve our todos from the API and display them.

Delete Request to Remove Todos

To delete a todo, we need to get the specific url for a todo item. We get that by appending the *todo.id* to the endpoint: *endpoint + todo.id*, e.g. *http://localhost:3000/todos/1*

Thus in *ToDoList*, in *onClick* of 'Delete', we specify the todo url, *endpoint + todo.id* to *axios.delete* to remove the todo:

```
          <td onClick={async () => {
                await axios.delete(endpoint + todo.id)
                dispatch({type:'delete',payload:todo})
          }}>Delete</td>
```

Because we use *await* on *axios.delete*, we need to specify *async* at the declaration of the function.

Run your app now and when you delete a todo, it will be removed.

Performing Post Request to Add Todos

Next, we will perform a post request to add a todo. In *ToDoList.js*, add the following codes in **bold**:

```
...
import { v4 as uuidv4 } from 'uuid';

function ToDoList(){
    ...

  const handleSubmit = async event => {
      event.preventDefault();
      if(editMode){
```

```
        dispatch({type: 'edit', payload:{...editTodo,text:todoText}})
        setEditMode(false)
        setEditTodo(null)
    }
    else{
        const newToDo = {id: uuidv4(), text: todoText}
        const response = await axios.post(endpoint,newToDo)
        dispatch({type: 'add', payload: newToDo})
    }
    setTodoText("")
}
...
```

Code Explanation

```
    else{
        const newToDo = {id: uuidv4(), text: todoText}
        await axios.post(endpoint,newToDo)
        dispatch({type: 'add', payload: newToDo})
    }
```

We will perform the post request in *ToDoList*; hence we should shift the creation of the new todo object from *todosReducer* in *App.js* to *handleSubmit* in *TodoList*. Thus, we move *import uuidv4* to *ToDoList.js* as well.

axios.post requires two parameters. The first parameter is the URL of the service endpoint. The second parameter is the object which contains the properties we want to send to our server. We thus call *axios.post* with our endpoint and the new todo object *newToDo*. And because we use *await*, we have to label *handleSubmit* as an asynchronous function with the async keyword.

We then dispatch the *add* action with *newToDo* as the payload.

Case 'add' in todosReducer

Next in *App.js*, *todosReducer*, in the *add* case, make the following changes:

```
case 'add':
    //const newToDo = {id: uuidv4(), text: action.payload}
    const addedToDos = [...state.todos,action.payload]
    return {...state,todos:addedToDos}
```

We remove the line to create *newToDo* as it's now created in *ToDoList* and passed as the payload. In *addedToDos*, we append the payload containing *newToDo* straight to the current todos in state.

Run your app and you should be able to add todos.

Performing Patch Request to Update Todos

Finally, let's implement editing a todo. Just add one line of code!

```
const handleSubmit = async event => {
    event.preventDefault();
    if(editMode){
        await axios.patch(endpoint+editTodo.id,{text:todoText})
        dispatch({type: 'edit', payload:{...editTodo,text:todoText}})
        setEditMode(false)
        setEditTodo(null)
    }
}
```

We call *patch* with the specific todo's end point and the attribute to be updated (in our case *text*). The rest of the code remains the same. And when we run our app now, we can edit a todo!

Slight Improvement

We can make a slight improvement to our app in terms of user interface because it is not obvious to the user that the *Edit* and *Delete* can be clicked (fig. 8.6).

Edit	Delete
Edit	Delete
Edit	Delete
Edit	Delete

Figure 8.6

Let's change them to button links as shown:

```
<tbody>
            {state.todos.map(todo =>(
                <tr key={todo.id}>
                    <td>{todo.text}</td>
                    <td onClick={() => {
                        setTodoText(todo.text)
                        setEditMode(true)
                        setEditTodo(todo)
                }}>
                        <Button variant="link">Edit</Button>
```

```
        </td>
        <td onClick={async () => {
            await axios.delete(endpoint + todo.id)
            dispatch({type:'delete',payload:todo})
        }}>
            <Button variant="link">Delete</Button>
        </td>
    </tr>
))}
</tbody>
```

When we run our app, *Edit* and *Delete* appear more visible to users that they can be clicked (fig. 8.7).

To Do	Edit	Delete
finishing writing hooks chapter	Edit	Delete
play with kids	Edit	Delete
Practise Piano	Edit	Delete

Figure 8.7

In case you got lost in any of the steps, here's the full code. Alternatively, visit my GitHub repository at *https://github.com/greglim81/react-hooks-chapter9*.

App.js

```
import React, { useReducer} from 'react';
import ToDoList from './ToDoList'

const todosInitialState = {
  todos:[]
};

export const TodosContext = React.createContext()

function App (){
  const [state, dispatch] = useReducer(todosReducer,todosInitialState)

  return (
```

116

```
    <TodosContext.Provider value={{state,dispatch}}>
      <ToDoList />
    </TodosContext.Provider>
  )
}

function todosReducer(state, action){
  switch(action.type){
    case 'get':
      return {...state,todos:action.payload}
    case 'add':
      const addedToDos = [...state.todos,action.payload]
      return {...state,todos:addedToDos}
    case 'delete':
      const filteredTodoState = state.todos.filter( todo => todo.id !==
action.payload.id)
      return {...state, todos: filteredTodoState}
    case 'edit':
      const updatedToDo = {...action.payload}
      const updatedToDoIndex = state.todos.findIndex(t => t.id ===
action.payload.id)
      const updatedToDos = [
        ...state.todos.slice(0,updatedToDoIndex),
        updatedToDo,
        ...state.todos.slice(updatedToDoIndex + 1)
      ];
      return {...state, todos: updatedToDos}
    default:
      return todosInitialState
  }
}

export default App;
```

useAPI.js

```
import {useState, useEffect} from 'react'
import axios from 'axios'

const useAPI = endpoint => {
  const [data, setData] = useState([]) // initial state empty array

  //To call data when component is mounted,
  useEffect(()=> {
    getData()
  },[])
```

```
  const getData = async () => {
    const response = await axios.get(endpoint)
    setData (response.data)
  }

  return data;
}

export default useAPI;
```

ToDoList.js

```
import React, { useContext, useState, useEffect } from 'react'
import { TodosContext } from './App'
import { Table, Form, Button } from 'react-bootstrap'
import useAPI from './useAPI'
import axios from 'axios'
import { v4 as uuidv4 } from 'uuid';


function ToDoList(){
    const {state, dispatch} = useContext(TodosContext);
    const [todoText, setTodoText] = useState("")
    const [editMode, setEditMode] = useState(false)
    const [editTodo, setEditTodo] = useState(null)
    const buttonTitle = editMode ? "Edit" : "Add";

    const endpoint = "http://localhost:3000/todos/"

    const savedTodos = useAPI(endpoint)

    useEffect(()=>{
        dispatch({type: "get", payload: savedTodos})
      },[savedTodos])

    const handleSubmit = async event => {
        event.preventDefault();
        if(editMode){
            await axios.patch(endpoint+editTodo.id,{text:todoText})
            dispatch({type: 'edit', payload:
{...editTodo,text:todoText}})
            setEditMode(false)
            setEditTodo(null)
        }
        else{
            const newToDo = {id: uuidv4(), text: todoText}
            await axios.post(endpoint,newToDo)
```

118

```
            dispatch({type: 'add', payload: newToDo})
        }
        setTodoText("")
    }

    return(
        <div>
            <Form onSubmit={handleSubmit}>
                <Form.Group controlId="formBasicEmail">
                    <Form.Control
                        type="text"
                        placeholder="Enter To Do"
                        onChange={event =>
setTodoText(event.target.value)}
                        value={todoText}
                    />
                </Form.Group>
                <Button variant="primary" type="submit">
                    {buttonTitle}
                </Button>
            </Form>

            <Table striped bordered hover>
            <thead>
                <tr>
                <th>To Do</th>
                <th>Edit</th>
                <th>Delete</th>
                </tr>
            </thead>
            <tbody>
                {state.todos.map(todo =>(
                    <tr key={todo.id}>
                        <td>{todo.text}</td>
                        <td onClick={() => {
                            setTodoText(todo.text)
                            setEditMode(true)
                            setEditTodo(todo)
                        }}>
                            <Button variant="link">Edit</Button>
                        </td>
                        <td onClick={async () => {
                            await axios.delete(endpoint + todo.id)
                            dispatch({type:'delete',payload:todo})
                        }}>
                            <Button variant="link">Delete</Button>
                        </td>
                    </tr>
```

```
            ))}
          </tbody>
        </Table>
      </div>
    )
}

export default ToDoList;
```

Summary

With this knowledge, you can move on and build more complicated enterprise-level fully functional React applications of your own!

Hopefully, you have enjoyed this book and would like to learn more from me. I would love to get your feedback, learning what you liked and didn't for us to improve.

Please feel free to email me at support@i-ducate.com if you encounter any errors with your code or to get updated versions of this book. Visit my GitHub repository at https://github.com/greglim81 if you have not already have the full source code for this book.

If you didn't like the book, or if you feel that I should have covered certain additional topics, please email us to let us know. This book can only get better thanks to readers like you.

Thank you and all the best for your learning journey in React!

About the Author

Greg Lim is a technologist and author of several programming books. Greg has many years in teaching programming in tertiary institutions and he places special emphasis on learning by doing.

Contact Greg at support@i-ducate.com.

Printed in Great Britain
by Amazon

10400646R00070